W0081835

HEART REHAB

HEART
REHAB

FINDING THE YOU
GOD CREATED YOU TO BE

JERRY FLOWERS JR.

WATERBROOK

WaterBrook
An imprint of the Penguin Random House Christian Publishing Group
A division of Penguin Random House LLC
1745 Broadway, New York, NY 10019
waterbrookmultnomah.com
penguinrandomhouse.com

All Scripture quotations, unless otherwise indicated, are taken from the Holy Bible, New International Version®, NIV®. Copyright © 1973, 1978, 1984, 2011 by Biblica Inc.™ Used by permission of Zondervan. All rights reserved worldwide. (www.zondervan.com). The "NIV" and "New International Version" are trademarks registered in the United States Patent and Trademark Office by Biblica Inc.™ Scripture quotations marked (KJV) are taken from the King James Version. Scripture quotations marked (MSG) are taken from The Message, copyright © 1993, 2002, 2018 by Eugene H. Peterson. Used by permission of NavPress. All rights reserved. Represented by Tyndale House Publishers. Scripture quotations marked (NKJV) are taken from the New King James Version®. Copyright © 1982 by Thomas Nelson. Used by permission. All rights reserved. Scripture quotations marked (NLT) are taken from the Holy Bible, New Living Translation, copyright © 1996, 2004, 2015 by Tyndale House Foundation. Used by permission of Tyndale House Publishers, Carol Stream, Illinois 60188. All rights reserved.

Copyright © 2025 by Jerry Flowers Jr.

Penguin Random House values and supports copyright. Copyright fuels creativity, encourages diverse voices, promotes free speech, and creates a vibrant culture. Thank you for buying an authorized edition of this book and for complying with copyright laws by not reproducing, scanning, or distributing any part of it in any form without permission. You are supporting writers and allowing Penguin Random House to continue to publish books for every reader. Please note that no part of this book may be used or reproduced in any manner for the purpose of training artificial intelligence technologies or systems.

WATERBROOK and colophon are registered trademarks of Penguin Random House LLC.

LIBRARY OF CONGRESS CATALOGING-IN-PUBLICATION DATA
Names: Flowers, Jerry (Pastor), author.
Title: Heart rehab / Jerry Flowers Jr..
Description: First edition. | New York, NY: WaterBrook, 2025 |
Includes bibliographical references.
Identifiers: LCCN 2025021874 (print) | LCCN 2025021875 (ebook) |
ISBN 9780593602911 (hardcover) | ISBN 9780593602928 (ebook)
Subjects: LCSH: Healing—Religious aspects—Christianity. | Self-love (Psychology) |
Love—Religious aspects—Christianity.
Classification: LCC BT732 .F595 2025 (print) | LCC BT732 (ebook) |
DDC 248.4—dc23/eng/20250711
LC record available at https://lccn.loc.gov/2025021874
LC ebook record available at https://lccn.loc.gov/2025021875

Printed in the United States of America on acid-free paper

1st Printing

FIRST EDITION

BOOK TEAM: Editor: Drew Dixon • Production editor: Jocelyn Kiker •
Managing editor: Julia Wallace • Production manager: Sandra Sjursen •
Copy editor: Tracey Moore • Proofreaders: Emily Cutler, Phil Newman

Book design by Mary A. Wirth

The authorized representative in the EU for product safety and compliance is Penguin Random House Ireland, Morrison Chambers, 32 Nassau Street, Dublin D02 YH68, Ireland. https://eu-contact.penguin.ie

For details on special quantity discounts for bulk purchases, contact specialmarketscms@penguinrandomhouse.com.

CONTENTS

INTRODUCTION

I don't want to be like this.

Have you ever been there? Have you ever thought to yourself, *I don't want to be bitter like this. I don't want to keep getting so angry. I don't want to feel like I'm not enough. I wish I could stop this spiral of negative thoughts.*

Nobody wants to stay stuck, yet how many of us keep thinking these or similar thoughts?

One of my greatest joys is seeing people grow. (I often say that I have the best job in the world—I get to wash feet for a living.) Several years ago, as I was conducting counseling sessions with church members, I noticed people sometimes struggled to hear the biblical truth in my sermons because of all the pain and trauma and abuse they had experienced. Then, an epiphany hit me like a 1996 Mike Tyson uppercut: As benevolent followers of Jesus, we can't accomplish certain things if we're not healed on the inside. For example, we're told, "Love your neighbor as yourself" (Luke 10:27). If you don't love yourself, you won't know how to love your neighbor.

So, around Christmas of 2021, I prayed for a vision of what to do in the next year. How could I best serve people? The Holy Spirit put in my heart to construct an online ministry called Therapy Thursday. It focuses on the inward work—whatever is strangling the Word and blocking someone's ability to hear next-level information because they're still haunted by horrors or terrors of the past. This book is the fruit and culmination of those Therapy Thursdays.

I've found that many people aren't faking being sick; they're faking being well! All of us deserve Oscars because we're so good at faking that we have it all together—myself included.

Basically, each of us is a compilation of three things:

1. What happened to us
2. What didn't happen to us
3. What we meditate or dwell on

Your personality, your perspective, your viewpoint, and your outlook—as well as the way you respond and the way you react to things—all stem from a combination of these three aspects. But before we dive into them, I want you to consider this question: Is it possible that the version of you that you became to survive is not the version God wants you to be?

Heart Rehab is all about healing the heart so you can be whole enough to love your neighbor as yourself. It's designed to cleanse your heart, your inmost being. You've already been washed by the blood of Jesus, but this book provides a washing of the heart so you can receive all the kingdom purposes you're designed to carry out.

Each of us needs to have the heart, the attitude, and the perspective to be kind to one another.

We all need healing on the inside.

We need *Heart Rehab*.

Let's get to work!

BONUS CONTENT

To continue rehabbing your heart, use your smartphone to scan the code for a bonus video diving deeper into the content of this chapter.

URL: waterbrookmultnomah.com/HRIntroduction

Penguin Random House collects and processes your personal information. See our Notice at Collection and Privacy Policy at prh.com/notice. This notice applies to this QR code and those used throughout this book.

HEART REHAB

ONE

THE PROBLEM IS
THE PATTERN

It happened after a while that the brook dried up, because there had been no rain in the land.

—1 KINGS 17:7 (NKJV)

When I was twenty-two years old, my mom did what I considered to be the evilest thing she could ever do. I'll never forget it because it changed my life.

Having just graduated from Texas Southern University, I wanted to make an impact on my generation, so I had launched my ministry as a Christian rap artist and found myself traveling quite a bit as a student pastor. That Friday night, two weeks after graduation, I ministered to several hundred high school and college students at a youth conference in Hutto, Texas. Since I had a two-hour drive back to Houston, I ended up going to bed around five A.M.

THE SOCK WE KEEP OVERLOOKING

A few hours later, at eight A.M., my mom stormed into my room and turned on the light. Can you believe that? She then had the audacity to wake me up by clapping and singing a song.

"This is the day, this is the day, that the Lord has made . . ."[1]

Look—I love the Lord. Our God is an awesome God. But what time did I go to bed after a long and fruitful day of ministry? And what time did my mom decide to become a human alarm clock?

To make matters worse, she spotted a dirty sock in front of her and picked it up.

"Jerry, your room looks filthy! You need to get up and clean this room. Look at all this stuff on the floor!"

I grew up in a household where my parents were strong advocates for cleanliness. When my mom made a bed, it resembled one in the showroom at Gallery Furniture. After she vacuumed, the carpet always had perfect lines. Everything in our home had to be immaculate. No dishes in the sink, no trash flowing over, the floor spit shined. This was my childhood.

"A wife is not going to like a dirty husband," my mom told me during my adolescent years. "Pick up your socks, Jerry. She might think you're cute, but no woman wants to deal with a filthy man."

On this particular morning, I wasn't thinking about my future wife. I was in a deep sleep—the drooling, mouth-wide-open kind—when Mom burst in, waking me up and telling me to pick up my dirty socks. And because I was exhausted and sleep deprived, I was more irritable. The flesh is more likely to win when you haven't had enough sleep, especially when the little you do get is interrupted by comments about your room and some socks on the floor.

1. "This Is the Day," paraphrased by Les Garrett, Scripture in Song, 1967/1980.

That's it. I'm moving. This is the last Saturday she's gonna come into my room and wake me up.

So, I got up, brushed my teeth and washed my face, threw on a backpack, and then went to find an apartment. After filling out an application and submitting my pay stubs, I got the key that day! That night I lay on the floor in my six-hundred-square-foot apartment and thought to myself, *Tonight I'm going to get some good sleep!*

But a weird thing began to happen just weeks after I moved in. My apartment started getting dirty. Saturday would come and I would look around and wonder how everything kept getting so cluttered. I had been trained to clean on Saturdays, so how come my apartment kept looking like this?

It was the shirt on my couch that I ignored on Monday.

It was the shoes in the middle of the floor that I ignored on Tuesday.

It was the pair of drawers I left by the closet on Wednesday.

It was the dish I left in the sink from a meal I ate on Thursday.

It was the sock I threw on the floor before taking a shower during the week—the sock I kept overlooking every day.

All of this led to me having a filthy apartment on Saturday. Eventually, I realized I had been getting mad at the wrong thing.

The problem wasn't my mother.

The problem was my patterns!

There I was, getting upset at my mother, but I ended up producing the same exact atmosphere in a different location.

Do you ever find yourself wondering how things inside you got so messy? How your mind got like this and how your attitude became so bad? Do you question why you're feeling angry or depressed? Why your words are so foul, why your relationships feel so chaotic, or why your lust has gotten so out of control?

Destructive patterns start with something as small as a sock.

It's not the flood that we should look at. It's the puddle. We need to consider the puddle days before the flood comes.

When a great ministry leader falls, it's easy to look at what they did at that moment. But really, it comes down to the countless bad decisions that led up to their fall.

So many times, we fear the fire but overlook the smoke. By fire I mean the absolute, obvious acts like having sex outside marriage or getting high. But what about the subtle things, like hitting the snooze button after you set your alarm for devotion time or not keeping your commitment to have date night every Tuesday with your spouse? Even though we claim we're not going to play with fire, we keep on inhaling smoke. Smoke is the dismissal or overriding of a standard or principle so you can engage in what you want. And we all know that smoke can kill you before a fire ever burns you, right?

Smoke is the sock we keep overlooking.

Sometimes a person gets mad at the situation in their life and decides that a change will solve the problem. "I'm gonna find me a new church," they say. "I'm gonna find me a new pastor and a new community." That's fine. But a new place does not veto God's old instruction. You can find a new pastor and a new church, but whatever God told you to do five years ago He'll still be telling you to do today.

Look at the problems we often find ourselves in. An overthinking problem is caused by a pattern of making projections about my future and preparing for them in my present.

A control problem? That's the desire to manipulate or command the outcome. It's the pattern of trying to control how something will go and how it will turn out.

Have a problem of often running away from something, or at least wanting to? That's the pattern of taking false escapes. Getting high is just a false escape. So is cheap sex. A pattern can form whenever you immediately try to find a temporary escape from anything difficult.

The shadow of every problem is the pattern.

Are you tired of seeing those messy socks day after day? Do you find your life in a habitual mess week after week? Do you keep trying to move away from your problems but find that they keep moving with you?

The problem is your routine.

THE POWER OR THE PROBLEMS

Every New Year's Day, gyms are packed with well-intentioned members. At the start of a new year, many churches have people in overflow. But how do those gyms and churches look in the middle of summer? It's easy to start strong but become frustrated when you don't see instant results. The same thing goes for our spiritual lives. The reason people quit praying is that they don't see their prayers working. Or maybe they get distracted or decide sleep is more important. Perhaps they convince themselves that they are too busy. Maybe they don't fast enough because they don't see that fasting works, at least not the way they want it to. But if we could see that our spiritual disciplines are working, then we might be more committed.

Experiencing the powerful blessings and favor of God often starts with our routines. A routine is "a sequence of actions regularly followed."[2] It can be cultivated either by discipline or by trauma, ignorance, or slothfulness. A routine is a commitment to the same.

What are the patterns and sequences in your life right now?

2. *Oxford Dictionary of English,* 2nd ed., rev. (2005), under "routine."

Do you find yourself constantly frustrated by not getting the results you want in life? The problem is in your routines.

The power or the problems in your life come down to your routines.

Some of us don't recognize the way trauma and pain are passed down through our bloodlines. How do problems become stronger and remain in your life for so long? How does trauma stick around? How does verbal abuse continue? How do poverty-minded spending habits remain? How do these things pass unnoticed from generation to generation, from baby boomer to Gen X to millennial to Gen Z? This happens because pain and trauma hide under the umbrella of normalized routines and patterns.

In other words, these patterns stay undetected because they are seen as normal. We repeat what we can't discern is broken.

Yes, mistakes hurt you. But the wrong patterns and routines can break you.

A KINGDOM ROUTINE

If you are a believer striving to grow in Christ, you're not just a Christian who likes Jesus. You are trying to be Christlike. So, when we look at Jesus, we can observe that He had routines. As I've said, the power or the problem is in the routine. Christ always showed the power in His routines.

Luke 5:16 says, "Jesus *often* withdrew to lonely places and prayed" (emphasis mine). Earlier, in Luke 4:16, Jesus "came to Nazareth, where He had been brought up. And *as His custom was,* He went into the synagogue on the Sabbath day, and stood up to read" (NKJV, emphasis mine). In these two passages of Scripture, we can already see that our King had routines.

Let's look at more examples from Luke.

"Coming out, He went to the Mount of Olives, as He was accustomed, and His disciples also followed Him" (22:39, NKJV). Here we see that Jesus was *accustomed* to going to the Mount of Olives, and His disciples followed Him. The genesis of discipleship is for you to show other people a kingdom routine.

"He was teaching daily in the temple. But the chief priests, the scribes, and the leaders of the people sought to destroy Him" (19:47, NKJV). This passage shows Jesus to be not just teaching but "teaching daily." The chief priests, scribes, and other leaders sought to destroy Jesus because mediocrity never celebrates excellence! Mediocre people hate excellence.

Jesus was taking the attention off them and showing the people the truth. "You don't necessarily need the Pharisees," His actions showed. "You need Me."

These passages are just a few of the many examples in Scripture demonstrating that Christ had routines. Jesus had patterns of teaching, of community, of discipleship, and of prayer.

Here's the quintessential question to ask yourself: *What is my routine?*

Some of you need new routines. So how is that going to happen?

New beginnings require old endings. If you want to truly say hello to something new, you have to say goodbye to something old. Why? Because the blessing of entry is tied to the sacrifice of exit.

Do you want to walk into God's light? You might need to exit something first. Will this be easy? Absolutely not. In fact, it's going to require a fight!

YOUR FOCUS MATTERS

Let's all pretend it's January 1. Sure, you might be reading this in the middle of August, but for now, let's assume that New Year's Day mentality.

This is going to be the year that my patterns change. This is the year for new routines.

Believe that this will be the year.

Believe that this is your moment, starting right now.

Believe that God is who He says He is and that He will do what He said He will do.

It's time to talk yourself into new patterns and routines. It's time to tell yourself exactly what you believe:

I believe I'm above and not below.

I believe I'm blessed going in and blessed coming out.

I believe that my past doesn't disqualify me because my God ensures that my destiny is greater than my disaster.

Do you truly believe those things?

What are the patterns in your life that you don't want to cross over into this new season? What bad attitude do you want to leave behind? How about the way you talk, particularly about other people? Or what about those bad relationships you find yourself in?

Just shouting in church won't ensure that these bad routines go away. It's going to require a fight! I might get hit, and I might even go down on the canvas. But I will get back up.

Changing a routine requires a fight.

It requires a fight for me to not dig up in doubt what I planted in faith.

It requires a fight for me to trust God's timing even when I think He's moving too slow.

It requires a fight for me to believe and know that I have an all-sufficient Savior who is not just watching me but is also with me right in the middle of my trials and storms, walking on the raging waters. And our God is so awesome that He doesn't just walk on the choppy waves—He invites me to come walk with Him.

Have you ever flown in an airplane and experienced turbulence? When that happens, do you find yourself paying more attention to the turbulence or to the distance you've traveled?

Which one do you tend to look at in your life: the turbulence or the journey? When you focus on the turbulence for too long, you don't even notice how far you've come.

Do you want to stop looking at the turbulence? Then it's going to require a fight. Not against people but against patterns that attempt to incarcerate the next-level version of yourself. It's a fight to stop normalizing dysfunctional routines and quit hanging onto fruitless patterns. Just because you're used to something doesn't mean it's healthy. God is trying to give us the key to overcome.

So, do you want this key? It begins with noticing how your unhealthy routines and patterns started in the first place. Deliverance is not just stopping the act; it involves discovering how the act started. Whenever you step out of a pattern because of its consequences without reprogramming, the enemy can always tempt you with old habits. This is why you keep going back. Yes, the year or location might change, like it did when I moved into an apartment, but that doesn't mean your routine will change.

The problem or the power is in the routine. Why do I keep saying that? Because I want this truth to stick in your mind like it's glued there. I want it branded on your heart.

The chain to your stronghold is in the routine.

The key to your spiritual growth is in your routine.

We are either stuck or growing because of what we keep doing daily.

The issue is not always Satan. We give him too much credit. Sometimes when we blame the devil, he's probably thinking, *I'm not even bothering you!* Instead, it's our detrimental routines that often lead to our demise. If we are in bad routines, Satan knows he doesn't have to revisit us for another four or five years. Our routines can be enough to steal and kill and destroy the stuff in our lives. We just need to fight to find the new powerful patterns.

What are some old routines in your life that you need to dig up and discard? What are some new, life-giving routines you can replace them with?

THE PLACE GOD REWIRES YOUR PATTERNS

"It's coming!"

We love to hear this in church, don't we? I often joke that if you are preaching and reach a bad point in your sermon or lose track of your notes, all you have to say are those two words. That's it. If I say, "Whatever you're praying about, it's coming!" people will start shouting.

But what if I tell you, "God is going to send you into the wilderness to deal with your pattern. It's coming!"?

All I'm hearing is silence.

Yet it makes sense why God would prescribe a wilderness for us, why He would create seasons of separation in our lives. It's because God wants to help us by dealing with our unhealthy patterns.

Let me give you a couple of examples, starting with the Israelites in Numbers 11:4: "Now the mixed multitude who were among them yielded to intense craving; so the children of Israel also wept again and said: 'Who will give us meat to eat?' " (NKJV).

Here's some context for this verse: At this point, the children of Israel have been delivered by Moses out of Egypt, and they're heading toward the Promised Land. They are going to the land "flowing with milk and honey" (Exodus 3:8), meaning it's agriculturally rich. But as they're traveling, the Israelites start to complain:

> We remember the fish which we ate freely in Egypt,
> the cucumbers, the melons, the leeks, the onions,
> and the garlic; but now our whole being is dried up;
> there is nothing at all except this manna before our
> eyes! (Numbers 11:5–6, NKJV)

What are the people essentially doing? They are demonstrating a pattern. They still remember the appetites they had when they lived in Egypt. Now they feel like their entire beings are drying up since they have nothing to eat except the manna God is giving them daily.

Sometimes we have nothing except what God uses to detox us.

What He uses to rewire our patterns.

What He uses to perform surgery on us.

The Israelites were left with nothing except God's changing of their appetites. What stands out to me in these verses is when they say, "Now our whole being is dried up." I feel as though God is asking each of us, "Can you recognize what I am trying to dry up in your life? Do you see that you're resisting My work because of your familiar pattern?"

The Israelites felt like they were being dried up. God was providing for them powerfully, but His provision was different from their pattern.

Again, what is God trying to dry up in your life, but you're resisting it because the new routine is not familiar?

So many times, we end up not at the place we desire in life but at the place we *crave*. We arrive not at the destination we long for but at the place our patterns take us. This is the reason a lot of us are struggling right now.

Struggling to get over it.

Struggling to break free from it.

No longer responding to it.

Not wanting to cry over it anymore.

The reason we feel so stuck with a posture, perspective, addiction, or thought pattern is that the problem is not the problem; the problem is the pattern. The problem is the appetite, the craving. Your non-detoxed heart is keeping a leash on your next-level self.

Let me say that again: An unregenerate heart is the leash that keeps any of us from experiencing the next level of ourselves, because former cravings won't allow us to embrace fresh manna.

The Israelites were complaining about the very thing God was using to train them and to give them another appetite. He had promised to take them to a land of milk and honey. That meant the manna was temporary. But they grumbled about the temporary season that God placed them in to address their pattern. They whined so much that they missed the Promised Land. They kept complaining even though God was so good that He gave them quail for meat and water from a rock.

How many of us hyper-complain because we feel the drying up of a pattern?

Former cravings won't allow us to embrace fresh manna.

Too often, we end up going to war with the wrong thing, thinking it's the problem. It's the pattern of the sock that you threw on the floor on Saturday and keep overlooking. But it isn't just that one sock. Changing the pattern means making sure to hang your shirt up every day and put your shoes away. It means throwing the water bottles in the recycling bin and washing the dishes every time you eat.

It's one thing to know what the problem is but another to know the knots that keep you from solving it—or perhaps that even strengthen its grip.

If you come out of a routine due to the repercussions but don't reprogram, the enemy can tempt you with meals from your "Egypt." When you're trying to stop some action, he might send people with that same pattern who try to get you to revert to the person you used to be or to relapse to the place God brought you out of.

This is why I'm so encouraged by you. Yes, you encourage me, dear reader, because the very act of picking up this book demonstrates that you are striving to be intentional with your healing. You are looking for scriptural guidance to grow and flourish. Your purposeful pursuit of healing is needed so Jesus can stem the flow of whatever in your life hurt you and left you bleeding. Your being *intentional* is assisting Jesus in making sure that the hemorrhaging stops, because He dries up patterns.

In Mark 5, a woman came to Jesus wanting to be healed. For twelve years she suffered with an issue of blood and had grown tired of doctors and people saying there was nothing she could do. She had spent all her resources. All she could do was pursue Jesus and touch the hem of His robe. Here's a part of the story we can easily overlook: "Immediately the fountain of her blood was dried up, and she felt in her body that she was healed of the affliction" (verse 29, NKJV).

What is God trying to dry up in your life? What will God dry up when you pursue Him and touch Him? When you seek His face? When you have a devoted life? When you have a consistent prayer life?

Is God trying to dry up something in your life, but you're resisting it because of the familiar comfort of a pattern?

Look at Elijah in 1 Kings 17 when God tells him to go "hide by the Brook Cherith" where he will be sustained (verses 3–4). But then what takes place? "It happened after a while that the brook dried up, because there had been no rain in the land" (verse 7). If Elijah's brook hadn't dried up, perhaps we never would have heard the story about his showdown on Mount Carmel. And he wouldn't have needed to ask the widow for food and then seen miracles happen.

If the sick woman who sought Jesus hadn't been intentional about her healing and then experienced something being dried up, we never would have known her story.

God will lead you to the wilderness. Why? Because this is the place where He rewires your patterns.

God wanted to rewire the Israelites' patterns. They still had an Egypt-minded appetite even though they had a Promised Land address. God wanted them to look not to Pharaoh anymore but to Him. He wanted to be experienced as Jehovah Jireh, the God who provides.

We should thank God for our wilderness season, because that is the place where God deals with our patterns. It is the place where He deals with those routines that need to be changed.

REHABBING YOUR HEART

Our routines are either the elevators or the undertakers for our spiritual growth. A routine is a commitment to doing the same thing for a season. Your life will begin to transform when you replace an unhealthy daily pattern with a healthy one and keep repeating it—because nothing changes if nothing changes.

Here are some routines that will help you in your spiritual growth.

1. Start with a routine of first and last

Give God the first and last of all you have. Begin and end each day with the words of Psalm 143:8:

> Cause me to hear Your lovingkindness in the morning,
> For in You do I trust;

Cause me to know the way in which I should walk,
For I lift up my soul to You. (NKJV)

At the start of the day, give God your first focus before you grab your phone. Do that the next morning too, and then repeat it every day. Before you close your eyes at night, go to the Lord and talk to Him. This is the routine of first and last.

Psalm 1:1–2 says, "Blessed is the man who walks not in the counsel of the ungodly, nor stands in the path of sinners, nor sits in the seat of the scornful; but his delight is in the law of the LORD, and in His law he meditates day and night" (NKJV). And when we do this, what happens? "He shall be like a tree planted" (verse 3, NKJV). Once you're planted, you know what happens? You bring forth fruit in season, and your leaf does not wither. And whatever you do will prosper.

It starts with the first and the last. This routine causes you to become planted and bear fruit—signifying stability and blessing.

2. Have a routine of preparation

Order is God's plan to simplify our lives.

Say that word out loud: "Order."

All of our lives need order. When you look at the creation narrative, God's brilliance exposes us to the pattern that He's a God of order. Before He created humankind, He made preparations. Man and woman came on the sixth day, and all the previous days were preparation. For example, God created the sun and the plants and photosynthesis. This is an example of how the circle of life happens. God didn't breathe life into Adam until He first made preparations that could sustain him.

What are you asking God to give you that your character can't sustain?

What are you asking God to do that you can't sustain emotionally?

What are you asking God to send that your sensitivity can't sustain?

Let's go back to that word again: *order.* God wants us to have order in our lives, and that means we must prepare and be practical. For instance, put gas in your car the night before a trip. Pick out your clothes ahead of time. Meal prep on Sunday morning so you can cook at home after church and won't stop at McDonald's or Starbucks.

Too many times, we like to say, "I'm not disciplined." But maybe the truth is you have no preparation. You will be more disciplined if you are prepared. That preparation—that routine— is one of God's means of bringing order to the chaos of your life.

3. Embrace the routine of grinding

We should have the work routine of grinding—being disciplined with a repeated task so that we experience results. Why is this important? It's because grinding is the part we play to ensure our due season.

Galatians 6:9 says, "Let us not grow weary while doing good, for in due season we shall reap if we do not lose heart" (NKJV). Don't be weary in well-doing. Don't let the grinding tire you out, for in due season you will reap a harvest if you keep going. Your grind is to ensure you'll do all right. All Christians are supposed to have five seasons, not four. The fifth is *due* season—that's when we experience the fruit of our labor. The only reason a lot of us haven't experienced our due season is because we have no routine of grinding, of working.

Never allow someone to cause you to question your grind when they don't have one. God didn't give them the vision for your life—He gave it to you!

4. Have a routine of rest

We all need rest. The routine of rest shows us that we must trust God for the outcome. Yes, we need to grind; we have to do our part. But then we need to rest. When you overwork yourself, you're saying to God, *I control the outcome.* You're saying, *God, I don't trust You. I really believe everything I do is up to me.* Yes, we have to work, because if we don't, we won't be able to eat (2 Thessalonians 3:10). But we should never work out of anxiety or fear of what's going to happen tomorrow (Matthew 6:34).

Rest shows that you trust God. Burnout doesn't always come because we're doing so much; rather, it can come because we're trying to give from a place of nothing. You won't invest well in others if you are running on empty. When we embrace our need for rest, we acknowledge our dependence on God and trust Him to restore us. At the end of the day, we need to do as Matthew 6:26 says: "Look at the birds of the air, for they neither sow nor reap nor gather into barns; yet your Heavenly Father feeds them. Are you not of more value than they?" (NKJV).

5. Employ the routine of temple care

Our bodies are temples of the Holy Spirit (1 Corinthians 6:19–20)—which means we should take care of them diligently and thoughtfully. And it is important to note that this applies not merely to our physical bodies but also to our mental, emotional, and spiritual selves. Temple care therefore refers to stewarding one's mental, physical, emotional, and spiritual self.

What does a routine of temple care look like? It can involve getting massages, working out, brushing your teeth, shaving . . . Don't laugh—I'm serious! You are carrying the kingdom inside you! Take care of it, and make space for activities that honor, heal, and care for your body. Make space for gym time. If you can afford it, make space for a regular massage. It's part of the routine of resting and being a wise steward of your temple.

Remember, if you don't make time for your wellness, you will be forced to make time for your illness. Too many of us wait until we are falling apart to start taking care of our bodies. Don't wait for a crisis to change your routine.

6. Enjoy the routine of reciprocity

How often do you return favors to other people? That is what the routine of reciprocity means. Maybe a friend pays for your lunch on Monday, so you offer to buy theirs on Wednesday. Maybe it looks like praising a colleague for their help on a project. Or maybe it's as simple as returning a smile to a stranger.

We need to have a routine of giving back. Be cognizant of those who give you a chance to let the Lord use you. This is about being generous not just with your money but also with your time, abilities, and wisdom. When God blesses you, ask yourself how you can display His love to others.

HEALING YOUR HEART

Sometimes when you read or hear a message like this, you wish you would have learned this idea of healing the heart sooner. We get so many emails, messages, calls, and letters to the church from people telling us, "I wish I would have heard this sooner in my life, because then I would have made different decisions."

I know how you feel. There are times when I pray, "God, if only I had known this, my choices would have been different." However, God recently shifted my perspective.

Instead of regretting that you didn't know something sooner, why not be proud of the person you were in the past? Be proud that you decided to keep going throughout your journey, because it led you to the place you are today.

This type of thinking frees me!

Be proud of who you were in the past, because you didn't quit! You didn't give up. You kept pursuing, kept learning. You kept going, and that's led you to this very moment. God wants you to see who you have been born to be!

QUESTIONS

1. What pattern in your life is God trying to dry up? Do you find yourself resisting His work because your routine is a familiar comfort?
2. Are you viewing certain relationships in your life in the wrong way? Are you mistaking the pattern as chemistry?
3. Are you excusing unhealthy patterns or aligning with any patterns by saying "This is just my personality"? Is it really?

PRAYER

Father, dry up any and every pattern that is not conducive to my purpose. Help me correct my actions before I create habits that don't lead me to the place I need to be for my purpose. In Jesus's name I pray, amen.

BONUS CONTENT

To continue rehabbing your heart, use your smartphone to scan the code for a bonus video diving deeper into the content of this chapter.

URL: waterbrookmultnomah.com/HRChapterOne

TWO

DON'T LOSE YOU

Before I formed you in the womb I knew you,
before you were born I set you apart;
I appointed you as a prophet to the nations.

—JEREMIAH 1:5

Have you ever considered that the shirt you're wearing right now was first somebody's idea? Think of your favorite pair of Jordan, adidas, or Gucci shoes. Or that red Fruit of the Loom T-shirt. Or maybe that favorite ugly sweater you can't give away. Before you ever purchased and wore them, these items were first in people's thoughts—designs swirling in their minds and waiting to come to fruition.

It's the same way with our own thoughts. You will eventually wear whatever you're thinking.

Our thoughts are apparel.

THE THREE YOUS

You will take on the nature of whatever you're thinking. That's why when your mind is filled with defeated thoughts, you will wear a defeated nature, even though that's not who you are. If you buy into the lie of being defeated, those thoughts become a version of you and displace the organic, God-made version of you.

So, if our thoughts are apparel, maybe you feel so discouraged because you're wearing your thoughts—or wearing others' thoughts. Like Proverbs 23:7 says, as a person "thinketh in his heart, so is he" (KJV).

We should never forget that you and I are wearing God's thoughts. He designed everything about you, including your skin. The Bible is full of passages that remind us that God knows us intimately.

In Psalm 139:1, the psalmist says, "You have searched me, LORD, and you know me."

God knows you.

In Exodus 33:17, the Lord told Moses, "I will do the very thing you have asked, because I am pleased with you and I know you by name."

God knows your name.

How long has God known us? Many of us are familiar with these words in Jeremiah 1:5: "Before I formed you in the womb I knew you."

God has always known you.

Can you see all of these yous? *I know you. . . . I know you by name. . . . I formed you in the womb.*

There is another *you* that comes from Jesus, and in my opinion, this is the scariest passage in the Bible. In Matthew 7:21–23, Jesus speaks this to the crowd:

> Not everyone who says to me, "Lord, Lord," will enter the kingdom of heaven, but only the one who does the will of my Father who is in heaven. Many will say to me on that day, "Lord, Lord, did we not

prophesy in your name and in your name drive out
demons and in your name perform many miracles?"
Then I will tell them plainly, "I never knew you. Away
from me, you evildoers!"

The first three passages deliver such hope: *I know you. I know
your name. I knew you before you were in your mother's womb.* But the
last passage is haunting: *Depart from me—I never knew you.* Doesn't
that last verse sound like a contradiction? But it's not. That's because it is possible for you to become someone God never created
you to be.

Maybe it's because of the culture.

Or your past.

Or your pain.

Perhaps some of you have become a you God never called you
to be. He has a plan for you, an assignment, a purpose. God has
promises for everyone, but some of us don't want them. Maybe
you don't want to trust Him. Instead, you believe other people's
lies and accept their false beliefs, and as a result, you become
someone you were never meant to be. You become the very thing
others have spoken over you. Sometimes we believe what others
say about us more than what God says about us.

Are you cloaked in insecurity due to the culture's definition of
beauty? That's not what God says is beautiful, but you're wearing
doubt because of what the culture says.

So, who are you? There are three different yous:

> The you that you're called to be
> The you that you used to be
> The you that you currently are

I want you to discover the you that God originally created you
to be.

When we stress ourselves out and feel like we're always so far behind in life, it's because we don't know how to trust that God is truly Jehovah Jireh, our provider. And then we can become other versions of ourselves. Or let me put it another way:

You can lose you.

Could you have lost the God-ordained version of you under the culture's lies? Under the pain of past trauma? Under the power of disbelief? The by-product of unhealed hurt is losing yourself.

We need to always remember that we are God-made. Waking up with this confidence is the gasoline that will fuel the rest of the day. But if we are not careful, we will allow our present anxiety to cause us to doubt our future. This anxiety can look like many things: betrayal, heartbreak, heartache, disappointments on repeat, and unfulfilled expectations.

When you look at your life, can you identify who you truly are? Are you the person God called you to be, or are you weighed down by another version of you?

Confused by all these yous? Let me explain by giving you an example. Often, depression happens when the real you has been pressed down. Perhaps the real you has been squelched by what your parents or the culture thinks about you, or maybe by trauma, your own expectations, divorce, church hurt, or addiction. Or perhaps it's been pressed down by the thoughts you continue to think about yourself. Remember, thoughts are apparel. Could it be that you are downcast and depressed because the *real* you has been stifled so much? Depression is a way of your spirit revealing that the real you has been pressed down.

Again, the by-product of unhealed hurt and unaddressed pain is losing yourself.

Let's take a look at the hurt and pain that we know as trauma.

MEDITATIONS BECOME MANIFESTATIONS

God is continually trying to develop each of us into the versions that He created us to be. But Satan wants to try to break us, and he uses the weapon of trauma to do so. One reason he wields the weapon of psychological abuse is that he wants us to keep wearing the apparel of what happened in the past.

Trauma is hell's attempt to bookmark your story.

Satan wants you to stay stuck. *You're not getting past this,* he whispers in your mind. *You're not going to the next chapter. You're never getting over this.*

You're going to wear this to the grave.

Yet while the enemy tries to detain us in the past, God is constantly trying to dress us for the future. He gives us reminders throughout the Bible. When the Israelites were in the wilderness, God told them He was dressing them for the future. He promised to bring them into the land that He swore to Abraham, Isaac, and Jacob, "a land with large, flourishing cities you did not build, houses filled with all kinds of good things you did not provide, wells you did not dig, and vineyards and olive groves you did not plant" (Deuteronomy 6:10–11). However, He also warned them to "be careful that you do not forget the LORD, who brought you out of Egypt, out of the land of slavery" (verse 12).

God wants us to never forget who has dressed us up for success. He is the one who prepares you for your purpose and dresses you for your destiny. But Satan wants to dress you in your former self so you'll keep wearing where you have been and what you have done.

It's so easy to normalize our trauma, isn't it? Some of your friends may wear their trauma. They talk about it, gossip about it, and never take it off such that it becomes part of their daily lives.

When trauma gets normalized, it robs you of the ability to

dream. You exchange your dreams for paranoia and constant overthinking of what might happen. Your dreams are replaced by doubts. And unaddressed trauma can move you to believe all the lies you've been told about yourself.

Is your mind constantly bombarded and harassed by those lies? What would it be like if you healed from this? What would life look like if you overcame that trauma? What would your testimony sound like if you could share where you had come from?

Hell wants you to never dream about how life would look if you were healed. That's because Satan is a mental assassin and psychological terrorist. And the main method he uses is to infect the motherboard of your meditations. The devil knows your meditations become manifestations. That's why he gives you thoughts in seed form—seeds of doubt, shame, anger, and so on. If you water those thoughts, they mature and transition from seeds into crops.

Satan knows how hard it is for God to use a person who believes his lies. But please hear this:

God can use you if you made mistakes or have an ugly past.

God can use you despite all your failures and your shortcomings.

God can use you even if you have made unwise, stupid choices like I have.

God can use you! He is not limited, but we refuse to let Him use us when we don't believe. That's it. Believing is the foundation of our faith. Receiving the gift of salvation is tied to confessing with our mouths and believing in our hearts that God raised Jesus from the dead (Romans 10:9). Satan wants to rob us of our ability to believe.

The enemy knows that God has given us an instruction that requires faith. He knows that faith is taking a risk and living like God is telling the truth about everything He has said. So, the devil gives us trauma, then reminds us about it and tries to keep us enslaved in it. He wants us to believe that we have gone through too much, that too many people have lied about us, and that too many have taken unfair advantage of us. So many of us don't take a risk of faith because our paranoia talks us out of it.

Normalized trauma robs you of your ability to dream and to have faith. And "without faith it is impossible to please God" (Hebrews 11:6). It's often the enemy who plants these thoughts that normalize our trauma.

So how can you prevent those seeds of doubt and despair from growing? How can you go to war against satanic thoughts and defeat them? How can you supervise your thoughts enough to engage in spiritual warfare when the enemy is telling you a lie?

The genesis of overcoming those lies and overturning the feeling of defeat is to remember who made you. Who is your father? Who is your creator?

You need to always remember this: *You have been tailor-made by God.*

I'M GOD-MADE

One January a few years ago, I was traveling to Minneapolis for a leadership and pastor's conference. At that time, the temperature there was -19 degrees Fahrenheit. Having been born and raised in Texas, I had never experienced the frigid temperatures that existed that close to the Arctic. So, as I prepared for the trip, I put on a thick coat and a scarf and mittens even though it was still 72 degrees in Houston. My sister couldn't believe it when she saw me.

"Boy, where are you going dressed like that?" she asked. "You're going to burn up!"

I gave her a simple reply: "I'm not dressed for where I am. I'm dressed for where I'm going."

What if we applied that same mindset to our lives?

I'm not staying in this defeated mindset.

I'm not staying in this fear.

I'm not staying in this resentment.

The fastest way for you to shake off defeat, shame, insecurity, and guilt is to engage in something I call Potter reflections (see Isaiah 64:8). These are times in your life when you pause to reflect on "What does the Potter say about me? What does my maker think about me?" This kind of reflection requires us to memorize Bible verses; then we can restate them when the lies start to come and the enemy tempts us to adopt those lies as truth.

Genesis 1:26 states, "Then God said, 'Let us make mankind in our image, in our likeness, so that they may rule over the fish in the sea and the birds in the sky, over the livestock and all the wild animals, and over all the creatures that move along the ground." Here, God the Father is talking to God the Son and God the Holy Spirit: "Let *us* make mankind in *our* image, in *our* likeness." This shows us that we are God-made, not man-made.

We live in a culture that loves the term *self-made,* as in a self-made millionaire or billionaire, a self-made champion, or a self-made hustler. But nothing about me is self-made. That is the culture talking. Everything about me is God-made. God made my heart, my mind, and my ministry.

Whatever I have in my life is all due to what God made.

I am God-made.

So, overcoming depression, self-doubt, self-abandonment, and self-rejection starts with remembering who made you. Again, you have been tailor-made by God.

Psalm 139:14 says, "I praise you because I am fearfully and wonderfully made; your works are wonderful, I know that full well." Once you know that you are God's work, it will enable you to begin to love yourself.

It's too easy for us to forget that we are created in God's image.

How do you destroy the reputation of a man or a woman? You mess up their image.

How do you sabotage the reputation of a ministry, corporation, or business? You mess up their image.

It's no wonder the enemy has been after you your whole life. It's because you are made in God's image. Satan figures if he can distort God's image by tarnishing humanity's image, then people won't look up anymore. The enemy loves to twist the way we look at ourselves so that we forget we were made in God's image. Satan loves to pervert the way we view and hear from God.

Do you ever feel like this? Do you ever wonder why it seems you can hear God but you can't see His work in your life? You start to think that something is wrong with you or the way you're looking at Him. Or maybe something is wrong with your mind or your personality.

That's what the enemy plants inside your mind. He wants you to think that it's your fault, not his, that your image of God is distorted. Never forget that we are wrestling "not against flesh and blood, but against the rulers, against the authorities, against the powers of this dark world," as Ephesians 6:12 states. It's not you—it's Satan trying to make you believe what you see.

I've messed up too much for God to use me.

This sort of thought is a falsified image of yourself. And a distorted view of yourself stems from a distorted view of God.

I'm ugly. You don't know the things I've done.

God counters this belief by saying, *You are fearfully and wonderfully made* (Psalm 139:14).

The reason you can't love yourself is that you've forgotten who made you.

Believing such lies from Satan doesn't just hurt you; it impacts all those around you. In Matthew 22:37, Jesus said to "love the Lord your God with all your heart and with all your soul and with all your mind." Then two verses later, He said to "love your neighbor as yourself." This is a biblical commandment. But how can you love others if you don't love yourself?

The problem is that it's hard to love others when you're coming from a place of drought.

Do you feel tired and burned-out with trying to love yourself and love others? Here is something to think about: Sometimes we burn out not because we're doing too much but because we're trying to give from a place of nothing. Your tank for loving yourself is empty.

Love the Lord my God with all my heart? I don't even know how to love me!

Love my neighbor like I love myself? That's impossible because I don't love me!

Do you walk around feeling angry? Do you spend the day in a state of joylessness? Maybe it's because you're exhausted and burned out from trying to give from a place of nothingness. Maybe you're waiting for somebody to discover you when you haven't even discovered yourself!

You have to learn how to love what God loves. And He loves you! God the Father loves you and wants to keep you, and He will never let you go. But we so easily forget this truth. We neglect to actively acknowledge that God is our Father and maker. If you don't love yourself, then you don't love the work of your maker.

The start of overcoming this place of emptiness and drought is to remember that we are tailor-made by God.

Growing up in church my whole life, I was repeatedly told to love God and others, but I was never told to love myself. I was not taught or trained or given a biblical framework for how to love myself. No one ever told me that it is a necessity and that it is not merely cultural—it is biblical.

So how do I love myself? How do I begin the journey of loving and knowing who God made me to be? How do I fall in love with the process of becoming versus shaming myself for who I've been? We must get to the place of loving what God loves.

Jesus once told a parable in which a son demands that his father give him his share of his inheritance (Luke 15:11–32). After receiving this, the son goes to a distant country where he spends his inheritance on riotous living. Eventually the son comes back, pleading with his father to make him like one of his hired servants. When you understand who God is, your prayers shift from "Father, give me my share of the inheritance" to a humbler "Father, make me as one of Your hired servants."

Many of us are familiar with how the father reacts when the prodigal son comes back, yet there is a specific detail that we may not notice. Verse 22 reads, "The father said to his servants, 'Quick! Bring the best robe and put it on him. Put a ring on his finger and sandals on his feet.'" The ring likely refers to a signet ring that identified the king's or family's legacy. Whenever a king signed a decree or an edict, he put his stamp on it with a signet ring.[1] So, in this parable, when the father puts the signet ring on his prodigal son's hand, he is reestablishing his son's authority and access to the family's legacy. Jesus is telling us that we have access to everything He has. We have access to His joy, His confidence, and His peace. We have access to healing through Jesus because He is giving us His stamp of approval.

The genesis of overcoming the feeling of defeat is remembering who your daddy is. When you remember how He loves you, you will start to love the work of His hands. And what is the work of His hands?

You.

You are handcrafted and singularly made by the loving Father who gives you access to everything He has.

1. Eitan Bar, "The Must-Know Meaning of the 'Robe,' 'Ring,' and 'Sandals' in the Parable of the Prodigal Son," Eitan Bar, eitan.bar/articles/parable-prodigal-son-robe-ring-sandals/.

DON'T LET FEAR KEEP YOU IN HIDING

What if you have already lost the you God wants you to be? Does that mean you are a lost cause? Absolutely not! But let me encourage you to do what you need to heal.

Have you lost the real you because people in your past hurt you? Because things happened that you can't seem to get over?

Or maybe you're hurt not because of what happened but because of what *didn't* happen. Did you place an expectation on people who let you down? Did you expect that something would have come about by the time you reached a certain age and now you're hurt because it didn't? Maybe you're hurt and upset because you gave God a deadline and He didn't meet your desire.

Are you carrying all this unaddressed pain? As I said before, the by-product of unaddressed pain is losing yourself.

Please hear me when I say you have to heal. You must heal because somebody needs the you that you've been called to be.

Your current or future spouse needs the real you, not the you that you used to be.

Someone in the community needs the version of you that you've been called to be.

What if I hadn't healed from my past hurts? I could not serve a single soul if I was still the person I used to be. Tell yourself the same thing I told myself: *Okay, I can't lose me. Yes, that betrayal hurt, but I can't allow it to press me down to where I lose myself. There's a generation who needs the called version of me.*

There's a generation, an audience, a platform, that needs the called version of you.

There's a household that needs the called version of you.

Somebody needs the kind of love that you cannot give until you become the called version of you.

And listen, the real you is not just one of many possible versions. It's the best, the most authentic version of you. It's the one that truly flourishes—the version of you that God intends you to be.

Yes, it's possible to lose yourself and go to a low place, but God created you for something else. He is the one to take you out of that desolate place and put you on a journey to become the you He wants you to be.

Let's look at someone in the Bible who was in a low place, living in the heart of trauma. In 2 Samuel, David had become king over Israel after Saul and Jonathan died. A custom of the day was that once a new king from a new family took the throne, they would kill off all the previous king's family to prevent a rebellion coming from a relative of the former ruler. This is the context surrounding 2 Samuel 4:4:

> Jonathan son of Saul had a son who was lame in both feet. He was five years old when the news about Saul and Jonathan came from Jezreel. His nurse picked him up and fled, but as she hurried to leave, he fell and became disabled. His name was Mephibosheth.

Fearing that soldiers were coming to kill Jonathan's family, a nurse caring for his son, Mephibosheth, tried to run away. But in her hurry, she dropped the boy, and he became permanently crippled. Later, King David wondered whether anybody was left in Saul's family that he could show kindness to for Jonathan's sake (9:1). When he asked this question of Ziba, a former servant of Saul's household, Ziba told David about Mephibosheth, Jonathan's son who was alive and lame in both feet. When the king asked where he was, Ziba answered that Mephibosheth was in a place called Lo Debar (verses 2–4).

But why is that important? Lo Debar literally means "no thing." If its name was any indication, Lo Debar was likely a wasteland, a desolate place with no pastures.[2] So, Mephibosheth went from being the king's grandson to being dropped and becoming hurt because a caregiver—someone he trusted—mishandled him. Now he was crippled in a place of nothing. But when King David had Mephibosheth brought to him, he surprised the younger man with this announcement:

> "Don't be afraid," David said to him, "for I will surely show you kindness for the sake of your father Jonathan. I will restore to you all the land that belonged to your grandfather Saul, and you will always eat at my table." (2 Samuel 9:7–8)

In response, "Mephibosheth bowed down and said, 'What is your servant, that you should notice a dead dog like me?'" (verse 8).

Look how Mephibosheth viewed himself: *How can you give an opportunity to a dead dog like me?* Does this sound familiar? Does that same voice ever speak inside your head? *Who am I to make a podcast? Who am I to start a YouTube channel? Who am I to begin writing that book? Who am I to raise these kids? Who am I to take on this project?* Mephibosheth was born into royalty, but he had lost the person he used to be because a caregiver dropped and injured him. This is childhood trauma at its finest. Somebody who was supposed to look after him, someone he trusted, ended up getting him hurt.

Have you ever been hurt by someone you trusted? Have those scars stayed with you and caused something inside you to shift? Maybe you view every potential caregiver now as somebody else with the potential of dropping and hurting you. That's what trauma does. Even when love knocks on the door of your heart,

2. "What Is the Significance of Lo Debar in the Bible?," Got Questions, gotquestions .org/Lo-Debar-in-the-Bible.html.

fear causes you to act like you're not home due to who dropped you.

The spawning pool of a judging heart is the unhealed trauma of being dropped or hurt several times.

Mephibosheth viewed himself as a "dead dog." But remember, David was a man after God's own heart. Here he reveals what God wants to do. *Is there anyone left in Saul's family that I can show kindness to?* David thought. *Whom can I show God's mercy, grace, and love to?* (See 2 Samuel 9:1.) When he finally met Mephibosheth, King David displayed God's goodness:

> Then the king summoned Ziba, Saul's steward, and said to him, "I have given your master's grandson everything that belonged to Saul and his family. You and your sons and your servants are to farm the land for him and bring in the crops, so that your master's grandson may be provided for. And Mephibosheth, grandson of your master, will always eat at my table." (verses 9–10)

This passage of Scripture is profound because it challenges us to start with the Lord—this is the first step to finding the you God wants you to be. It's literally going to your Designer and seeing how He designed you in the first place.

FINDING THE YOU THAT YOU ARE MEANT TO BE

The first step in the journey of discovering the you God has cosmically created you to be is to go to the One who made you. You're not going to find the God-ordained version of you in anything else outside Him. Of course, this starts with accepting Christ as Lord.

So, why do so many of us who are in Christ still feel lost? Do you ever feel like this? Yes, you know you are in Christ, but you have lost yourself.

I use an analogy to illustrate this. Say I put a picture of me as a child in the bottom of a trash can. Then I cover it with a bunch of *stuff*—the picture is still there, but it's buried under all that garbage and refuse. As a believer, you're not lost anymore, but maybe you've buried the real you under intense pain and false beliefs and burdens. Unlearning abuse looks like digging through the trash to redeem that child.

So, after accepting Christ, the second step to redeem the you that God created you to be is to come out of Lo Debar. Come out of the place of nothing. Recognize the things in your life that leave you with nothing. Remember, Lo Debar is a wasteland, a place with no pastures.

What in your life is contributing to waste?

What is a drain instead of a fountain?

What is a weight rather than a lift?

Identify what in your life is causing you to stay in a place of nothing.

God wants to bring you out of that place of desolation. As James 4:8 states, "Draw near to God and He will draw near to you" (NKJV). He says that if you come to Him, He will come to you. So, the first thing is to find the Lord and come out of those places that contribute to nothing.

The next step in finding the God-designed you is to forgive both others and yourself. I promise you, bitterness always handcuffs the God-ordained version of you. Bitterness contaminates the container. We must recognize that forgiveness isn't saying that what others did was right; it's saying that we choose to not be held captive due to those wrongs. When I don't forgive someone, I install the offender as my prison warden; only they can get me out of this jail. That's why you have to forgive. You must also forgive yourself. Why? Because the original version of you is not worth being incarcerated. God wants you to come out of Lo Debar.

Another step to discover the you God created you to be is to formulate your vision. When you don't have a forward vision, you will revert to familiar chaos. Chaos is addicting for those who have been born in it. You might not even realize this, but dysfunction is chaotic. So, you must get to a place where you can develop a forward vision. Ask yourself, *Where is God taking me? Where am I going?*

Release what happened, and ask yourself where you must go. It's so easy to focus on the *what* for healing purposes: This is *what* happened. This is *what* I heard. This is *what* crippled me. Yes, we have to acknowledge all that, but we can't stay there. We have to formulate the *where*. We need to heal from what happened so we can get to where we can serve people again.

A fifth step in finding the true you is to guard your ears. You are most vulnerable to injury after surgery. So, while God is redeeming the you that you lost, be careful who is speaking into you. With natural surgery, you might need somebody to drive you home from the hospital and help you so you don't injure yourself again. It's the same with the spiritual procedure of discovering who God created you to be. You need to guard yourself against reinjury, which in this case often comes in the form of who's talking to you.

The last step is to rehearse affirmations. If I keep telling myself that I'm a dead dog, then I'll believe that lie. As I said, thoughts are apparel. So, what are you thinking about yourself? We must know and rehearse God's thoughts about us and be affirmed in them. The following are examples of some scriptural truths about you that you can tell yourself:

What I carry is not a receipt of my value.

When God made me, He had no eraser because He makes no mistakes.

Nothing in this world designed me, so nothing in this world can define me.

Remember that loving yourself is nothing more than cherishing the work of the Potter. How you view you is the syllabus for how you'll expect others to treat you. When you view yourself as royalty, you won't allow yourself to be treated like trash. Loving yourself means cherishing the Potter's craftsmanship.

Always remember that you are God-made. When He made you, He had no eraser, because God makes no mistakes.

QUESTIONS

1. In what areas of your life have you lost sight of who God created you to be? How might these areas be affecting your relationship with God and others?
2. What voices or experiences from your past have shaped how you view yourself today? Which of these align with God's truth about you, and which need to be replaced?
3. How can you begin to incorporate Potter reflections into your daily life? What specific Scripture verses speak to your true identity in Christ?
4. What practical steps can you take this week to rediscover and embrace the authentic version of yourself that God designed you to be?

PRAYER

Father, would You help me come out of the place of nothing? Give me the strength to forgive others and forgive myself. Some of them didn't know what they were doing. And some, including me, did know. But if You can forgive me, surely I can forgive myself. When I forgive, I look more like You. Father, I thank You that You're helping me establish a forward vision so I won't revert back to chaos. Show me how to guard my ears so I can rehearse your affirmations versus the culture's and the enemy's lies. In Jesus's name I pray, amen.

BONUS CONTENT

To continue rehabbing your heart, use your smartphone to scan the code for a bonus video diving deeper into the content of this chapter.

URL: waterbrookmultnomah.com/HRChapterTwo

THREE

IT STARTED IN CHILDHOOD

He got up, took the child and his mother during the night and left for Egypt, where he stayed until the death of Herod. And so was fulfilled what the Lord had said through the prophet: "Out of Egypt I called my son."

When Herod realized that he had been outwitted by the Magi, he was furious, and he gave orders to kill all the boys in Bethlehem and its vicinity who were two years old and under, in accordance with the time he had learned from the Magi.

—MATTHEW 2:14–16

There is a dark room inside each heart that many of us have never fully addressed. It's locked tight by memories too painful to confront, by wounds we're still afraid to touch.

It's the room where childhood trauma resides.

One of the enemy's most potent weapons against our generation—and the generations before and after—is the trauma we carry from our earliest years. He aims it not just at our bodies but also at our souls. Childhood trauma is the devil's attempt to rob us of our potential before we even know we have it.

WHAT IS NOT REHABILITATED
WILL BE RECYCLED

In chapter 2, I talked about how Satan wants us to stay stuck in our broken past and how trauma is his attempt to bookmark our stories. In this chapter, I want to dive deeper and have a heart-to-heart conversation about this powerful weapon the enemy wields. This weapon, often deployed early in life, has a strategic purpose. I believe hell uses childhood trauma for two primary reasons: to prevent us from maturing and to give our wounds generational momentum.

So many of the hurts that form our foundations and the wounds we carry into adulthood started at home. Maybe it was the absence of a father or the cruel words of a mother. Maybe it was neglect or even abuse. The enemy knows if he can distort your view of your earthly father, he can distort your view of the Heavenly Father. This is why hell is after our men—our fathers, sons, and brothers—because when a father breaks his child's heart, that child may grow up unable to trust anyone, including God. The word *father* itself can become a trigger—when we speak of the love of our Heavenly Father, it feels foreign to those who have never experienced that kind of love on earth. The enemy knows that a twisted image of God the Father will delay spiritual maturity and keep us in a cycle of distrust and disbelief. What hasn't been healed will be recycled.

In this chapter, I will break down three critical aspects of childhood trauma:

> What is the weapon of childhood trauma?
> Why does untreated trauma blur discernment?
> How do we heal from the dark room?

IMMATURITY ECLIPSES THE MATURE
VERSION OF YOU

Consider the story of Herod. This chapter's opening Scripture passage, Matthew 2:14–16, offers us a glimpse into the escape of Jesus and His family from Herod's murderous rage at being outwitted by the wise men.

The enemy used Herod to commit genocide with one goal in mind: to prevent the maturation of the future King, the deliverer. Satan knew that this young child would one day pose a great threat. Therefore, the assault had to happen before maturity could set in. Childhood trauma functions the same way. The enemy aims to keep us spiritually, emotionally, and mentally stunted, ensuring we never become the people God has destined us to be.

In verse 13, Joseph was warned in a dream to take his family and flee. But what happens when there's no escape? What happens when the family meant to protect you becomes part of your wounding? What do you do when the people entrusted with your safety—the ones who should have helped you flee your own "Herod"—were complicit in your pain? For many of us, the families that should have shielded us handed us over instead. That's the reality of childhood trauma.

We shouldn't miss the message in the story of Herod: The enemy wants to kill a deliverer and a coming king. He wants us to never reach maturity so we'll never become an issue. *If I don't attack them in childhood*, the devil thinks, *they will become my problem later*. So, he uses childhood trauma as a security deposit.

Hell wants us to never mature.

What happens in childhood may not feel relevant either then or now, but if it goes unaddressed, it can affect us when we least expect it. Our unresolved wounds can begin to manifest in dysfunctional ways.

The enemy fears our growth. He knows that when we think, respond, and live with maturity, we become dangerous to the kingdom of darkness. Spiritual maturity equips us to handle adversity differently. Instead of reacting out of fear or hurt, we begin to walk in wisdom and grace. We no longer need validation from our pain, and we stop seeking approval from unhealthy sources. Maturity transforms us from victims to victors, and hell trembles at that transformation.

Mature people evolve. They break cycles, heal, and grow. The enemy's strategy is to interrupt that evolution. One way we can identify distractions or counterfeit relationships is by examining whether they attempt to hinder our growth. A distraction doesn't mean you can't focus; rather, it's any person, place, or thing that mismanages your focus. It deviates where your focus should be. A counterfeit is something that appears to be real but, after closer inspection, turns out to be fake.

If a relationship pulls you away from your evolution of healing and growth, it's not from God. The enemy uses distractions and counterfeits to keep us from evolving into the mature individuals God has called us to be.

Remaining in a state of immaturity is hazardous because it eclipses the version of yourself that God intends to use for His kingdom. Many of us become comfortable in our immaturity because society and even our spiritual environments don't challenge us to grow. We can end up doing the bare minimum as believers. The only time we might think about God is on Sunday mornings, and often we remain stuck because of sugarcoated messages that make us feel good but don't push us toward transformation.

Satan doesn't just want to wound us for our lifetimes. He also wants us to pass those wounds down through our bloodlines. If a trauma goes unhealed, it gets transferred to the next generation, creating a cycle of pain that can last indefinitely. We end up fighting wars that don't even belong to us—unfinished battles from our parents or grandparents. The same Goliaths that attacked them now stand in our paths because we inherited wounds that were never healed.

If we don't transform our pain, we transfer it.

TRIGGERS ARE THE ENEMY'S CHECK-IN DATES

So many of us carry something that I call *traumatic aloneness.* For example, say you were six years old and were left alone longer than you should have been. One night your mother said she would be back in an hour, but one hour became two and then three. After several more hours, as the sun was coming up, she finally walked back in. This moment traumatized you.

For others of us, that parent never returned. Maybe you were seven when your father left you and your mother alone and never came back. Many birthdays have passed, and now you're grown but wonder why you can't stand being alone. It's because of traumatic aloneness. So, when God calls you to a season of separation, you're triggered because it takes you back to when you were that scared child on your own.

The enemy loves to trigger you, taking you right back to your most traumatic events. It's what he uses as his check-in date to live rent-free in your head and emotions. Those triggers are suffocating your obedience. Your gift and your calling can be strangled if you don't allow God to heal the things that set you off.

Have you become one with your triggers? Maybe it's not your boss or your spouse who is the issue; maybe the trigger existed long before them. And those triggers are strangling your ability to fully obey God.

TRAUMA PLAYS HAVOC WITH OUR CALLINGS

Why does childhood trauma have such a lasting effect? Trauma blurs discernment. When we don't address our past pain, it clouds our ability to hear from God clearly in the present. Our wounds begin to speak louder than the Holy Spirit. Instead of trusting God's voice, we listen to the voice of our pain, fear, or insecurity. This distorted discernment makes it difficult to determine whether God is guiding us or we are simply reacting to our wounds.

Trauma trains us to protect ourselves. God designed us to connect, but trauma rewires our brains for self-preservation. This is why unhealthy relationships, or entanglements, often feel safe—they play into our need to protect ourselves from further hurt. However, this protective stance often leads us further from God's will for our lives because it makes it difficult to trust others or receive healing.

When we are so used to making decisions based on protecting ourselves, we become suspicious of even the people God sends to help us. We view every kind word or act of love as a potential threat because we are operating from a place of untreated pain. This is why trauma is so damaging—it twists our view of reality and prevents us from discerning God's will clearly.

Trauma prevents us from being the world changers God created us to be.

In life, there are moments when you feel set apart, different, or even targeted in ways that seem unexplainable. These can be indicators that God has marked you as a world changer. Let's explore some of these signs and how they manifest in your life.

1. Being assaulted before you're mature

One of the clearest signs that you've been marked by God is that you face spiritual opposition before you've matured. The enemy will often attack you as a child (in the natural or the spiritual) because he is terrified of what you're going to become. These early challenges are not random; they are a clear indication of the potential that lies within you. The devil seeks to prevent you from realizing your calling before you have a chance to step into it.

2. Being the different one in the family

Another indicator you are set apart for something great is being the different one in your family. Perhaps you are the one who recognizes dysfunction where others may not. While your family may be engaged in patterns or behaviors that seem normal to them, you have the ability to see things clearly. But this difference is significant because you are the one chosen to bring change.

Maybe you're the only person in your family who doesn't get drunk. The only one who doesn't sleep around. The only one who goes to church. The only one who goes to therapy. Where others are trapped in dysfunction, you are the oddball that's going to break the cycle.

3. Resisting peer pressure

As a world changer, peer pressure likely didn't have the same hold on you as it did on others. You never felt the need to conform or do what everyone else was doing. There was always something about you that didn't quite fit in with the crowd. It may have taken time, but eventually, you realized why.

You weren't made to follow the current. You were made to go upstream.

4. A wrong introduction to God

Another indicator you have been marked by God is when you have had a wrong introduction to God. This is also a tactic of the enemy, aiming to skew your view of the Father and prevent you from seeking a closer relationship with Him. The enemy wants you to believe a lie about God so that you never desire to know Him fully. He doesn't want you to come to understand the truth and strive to build a genuine relationship with the Father.

5. Separation for a purpose

Lastly, you know you have been marked by God to be a world changer when you have been separated. A lot of us mislabel separation as loneliness. You're not lonely—you're separated. God is setting you apart for a unique purpose.

Let's go back to the idea of traumatic aloneness. Sometimes God wants you to have solitude not because He's punishing you but for the purpose of training you to know His voice. But you're triggered from it. It takes you back to that six-year-old girl wondering when your mother's going to come back. She said she was going to the store, but she was really going to another man's house. It takes you back to that seven-year-old boy whose father told him he was going for a haircut and never came back.

Don't mislabel this time of separation. You are being prepared, molded, and transformed into the person you are called to be.

HEALING IS THE ABILITY TO ENDURE THE SEASON OF NOT YET

Now that we have covered how the enemy uses trauma against us and why it blurs our discernment, the natural question that follows is how we heal from childhood trauma. How do we escape these dark rooms that have held us captive for so long? The devil may have tried to break you in childhood, but God is here to redeem your story. The question is, Will you let Him?

God wants to heal your inner child. The process of healing is often uncomfortable, however, because it involves confronting old wounds and unresolved trauma. God is less concerned with your immediate happiness and more focused on making you whole. But this procedure can feel like you're under construction. God uses a wrecking ball to break down the bitterness, false beliefs, and unhealthy patterns you've learned over time. It's painful but necessary. There is a person you are meant to become. There's a life you're meant to live and likely a spouse you're meant to love. But first, the old structures must be torn down to make way for the new.

How do you move forward from here? How do you overcome deeply ingrained patterns and step into the fullness of what God has called you to be? Here are several steps to guide you on this journey:

1. Deal with the untold stories

The first step is to confront the untold stories—those painful memories we've buried and tried to ignore. These stories haunt us internally, and even though we might not talk about them, they shape who we are. When we fail to deal with our childhood wounds, they rob us of our authenticity. And confidence is tied to authenticity. When we pretend the trauma never happened, we lose touch with who we truly are, making it impossible to live with confidence.

It's time to shine a light on that dark room.

It's time to bring those untold stories to the surface.

You cannot be who God created you to be while carrying the weight of unresolved trauma. Healing starts with being honest with God, yourself, and others about the pain you've experienced. When we give God our wounds, He heals them.

2. Forgive the teacher

One of the most critical aspects of healing from childhood trauma is realizing that the problem often is not with the people in your life but with the patterns they are caught in. Many times, we place blame on individuals, thinking they are the source of our pain or struggles. The truth is, a destructive pattern may have existed long before these people entered our lives. The people merely became part of the cycle, not the cause of it.

Recognizing this distinction is vital to your healing process. You're not just breaking up with a person; you're breaking up with a pattern that has bound them. Once you see this, you can begin to address the root issues rather than continue to blame individuals for things they may not fully understand themselves.

Many of the lessons we learned early in life came from our first teachers—our parents, friends, and family. Sometimes they taught us wrong because they, too, were taught wrong. It's important to forgive them for the incorrect lessons and to recognize that they did the best they could with what they knew. This doesn't excuse the hurt, but it allows you to release it and move forward.

3. Forgive yourself

Healing means we must be willing to forgive not only those who hurt us but also ourselves for the mistakes we made as a result of our pain. This doesn't mean excusing harmful behavior; rather, it means releasing the grip that pain has on us. Forgiveness is not about letting anyone off the hook; it's about freeing ourselves from the prison of bitterness. You were in the dark, but now you see more clearly. Release the guilt, and embrace the truth.

If God is willing to forgive us, why shouldn't we? Don't be harder on yourself than God is.

4. Embrace rehab

The process of healing, or rehab, is about retraining your mind and spirit. As Proverbs 22:6 states, "Train up a child in the way he should go: and when he is old, he will not depart from it" (KJV). This principle applies to your inner child as well. If your inner child is in a dark room, you may not even recognize that in this very moment, God is trying to train that child.

5. Rehearse new affirmations

Romans 10:17 says, "Consequently, faith comes from hearing the message, and the message is heard through the word about Christ." Begin to speak new affirmations over your life. Replace the destructive lies you've learned with God's truth:

I'm the head and not the tail.
I am above and not beneath.
I will live and not die.

These affirmations will help rewire your thinking and strengthen your faith.

6. Be patient with the process

You must learn patience. Healing takes time, and patience is the ability to endure the season of *not yet*. Trust God's timing, and embrace the process, knowing that God is working for your good.

As you embark on this journey of healing and transformation, remember that God is shining a light on the dark rooms of your life. He is giving you the keys to escape, to forgive, and to grow. Trust the process, and embrace the work He is doing in you.

THE BLOOD IS STRONGER THAN THE MUD

As a church, we need to have conversations about childhood trauma and abuse. Too many people feel dirty even though they never played in the mud. The trauma they suffered as children has kept them in dark rooms of guilt and depression. Why aren't we addressing their struggles?

Do you feel guilty and dirty for things you didn't do or situations you couldn't control?

Jesus's blood is stronger than the mud.

Romans 5:9 states, "Since we have now been justified by his blood, how much more shall we be saved from God's wrath through him!"

What does it mean to be justified? God chooses to treat us as if we didn't sin. God justifies us through the blood of Jesus; His blood ensures that we are forgiven. Jesus was wounded for our transgressions, and He was crushed for our iniquities (Isaiah 53:5–8). The stuff in the dark rooms—the issues we haven't told anyone about—His blood works for that too.

Ephesians 1:7 says, "In him we have redemption through his blood, the forgiveness of sins, in accordance with the riches of God's grace." To be redeemed means to be bought back. The blood of Jesus purchased us and brought us back into a proper relationship with the Father. We have redemption through His blood.

What else does the blood do? The blood gives us power over the enemy. Revelation 12:11 says that followers of Jesus have "triumphed over [the devil] by the blood of the Lamb and by the word of their testimony; they did not love their lives so much as to shrink from death."

Jesus's blood helps us overcome the enemy.

His blood still works.

All of us who are in dark rooms of childhood trauma have been blood-bought by God.

Healing is a journey, not an overnight transformation. It takes time to untangle the wires that trauma has twisted in our minds and hearts. But the good news is that God is patient and that He walks with us every step of the way. We may be in dark rooms right now, but God has the power to turn on the light.

As we move forward, remember this: The dark room of childhood trauma is not where your story ends. God's desire is for you to mature, evolve, and break the generational cycles of pain. You are dangerous when you pursue maturity because you become a threat to the kingdom of darkness. When you heal, you not only set yourself free; you set the next generation free.

QUESTIONS

1. What childhood experiences might be affecting your spiritual growth and maturity today? How has this impacted your ability to trust God?

2. How has the enemy used childhood trauma to bookmark your story? What page is God wanting to turn to in your life right now?

3. Which of the five indicators that you've been marked by God resonates most with you? How might God be using your past pain for a greater purpose?

4. What steps can you take to begin healing from your childhood wounds? Who might God be placing in your life to help with this healing process?

PRAYER

God, I pray right now that You'd shine a light on the dark room of childhood trauma. Help me learn how to escape this dark room. Please allow me to forgive anybody that taught me the wrong way—my parents, professors, friends, and family members. As I embrace this journey of rehab, help me run and detox so that I can become a servant for Your kingdom. I pray this in Jesus's name. Amen.

BONUS CONTENT

To continue rehabbing your heart, use your smartphone to scan the code for a bonus video diving deeper into the content of this chapter.

URL: waterbrookmultnomah.com/HRChapterThree

FOUR

YOUR MIND IS TOO CROWDED

Do not conform to the pattern of this world, but be transformed by the renewing of your mind. Then you will be able to test and approve what God's will is—his good, pleasing and perfect will.

—ROMANS 12:2

There was a time in my life when every Saturday night turned into an anxiety session. I found myself so tired of waging war with my questions and fears about the coming Sunday morning:

Will this sermon be spiritually nutritious?
Part 4 was good, but how is part 5 going to be?
What illustration should I use tomorrow? I just used that one last week.
Will this sermon help anyone love Jesus?
Am I really living faithfully in line with what I am about to preach?

I would tell my wife, Tanisha, how weary I was of dealing with these anxious thoughts. On one particular Saturday evening, I cried out to the Lord.

"God, I don't want to preach anymore," I prayed. "If this is what my Saturdays are going to look like for the rest of my life or until I go on sabbatical or pass the ministry on to my successor, I don't want to preach!"

The thought of enduring this war every single weekend for the foreseeable future was overwhelming. I was tired of the anxiety and the overthinking, tired of the wondering and the questioning. One day while I lay prostrate on the floor, crying out to God for help with this, the Holy Spirit gave me a word that changed my life forever.

This is not anxiety, the Holy Spirit told me. *This is the fear of the Lord.*

A peace instantly hit my heart as a heavy weight lifted. I was so worn out that I hadn't realized I was mislabeling anxiety.

What are you labeling as an anxiety issue that is really a campus where God wants to teach you something?

This is why we need Jesus *and* therapy. Had I taken my so-called anxiety to a therapist who was not Spirit-led, they would have simply given me strategies on how to overcome anxiety and a list of steps to defeat my fears. They probably would have been well intentioned, with their heart in the right place. And since I'm a man of discipline, I would have tried to figure out those steps and followed the routine. But God gave me another message:

This is not anxiety. This is the fear of the Lord, He told me. *This is you realizing how much you need Me—that without Me you'll fail. Don't label it something else.*

The truth is, I can't even think of trying to get on a stage without the Lord. I'd be terrified to preach without His presence. I fear doing anything on my own, and I'm honest enough to admit that I would look foolish without Him. So, I prayed a new prayer:

"Lord, I don't know what I'm doing without You! I don't know how to husband or how to pastor without You. I know I can't father or mentor or friend or family without You. So, lead me beside still waters. Please, Lord, shepherd me."

The Holy Spirit had spoken the words of Proverbs 9:10 over me: "The fear of the LORD is the beginning of wisdom, and knowledge of the Holy One is understanding."

Any wisdom that has come from my ministry, whether spoken from a pulpit or on a podcast, has not come from my own efforts. Any level of spiritual intelligence during Therapy Thursdays has not come from the degrees I've earned or from my hours of study. Those are just ornaments; they're not the core.

The nucleus of the wisdom being poured on me is the fear of God.

What if some of the trials or difficulties that you've flagged as problems, like I did, are actually a university in which God is trying to teach you something?

I wasn't battling anxiety every Saturday night. Those thoughts were an insurance deposit to keep me from losing my sense of desperation for God or finding success apart from Him. To ensure that I never start thinking that I'm doing this on my own. To always give God the glory, because without Him, I'm terrified. Those moments were reminders that I never want to preach without God's presence. Every service, I want Him to breathe on our encounter.

To fail to learn from that deposit would be arrogant. Some people who find success forget who gave it to them in the first place. But God gently whispered to my heart, *Jerry, you're keeping that fear for Me.*

It was so easy to stamp "anxiety" on this situation. Our society does this all the time—putting a label on something that is hard to overcome. Anything that doesn't fit in or doesn't follow the routine immediately gets tagged. "This is how you think? Here's a label. This is hard for you? Here's another one."

Here's the thing: Once a label gets married to identity, we become one with it.

When our parents or caregivers don't really understand us,

they label us. Think back to your childhood. Did you ever hear a statement like one of these?

> "You're just like your dad. You never follow
> through on your promises."
> "Your problem is you never listen."
> "Why can't you be more like your sister? She is
> always on top of things."
> "You are such a troublemaker."

Labels can stick all over you and never come off.

There is a connection between never being understood and overthinking. Some of you who were misunderstood began to overthink and wonder what was wrong with you. Doubt has clouded your mind with questions ever since:

Why am I like this?
Why do I feel like this?
Why do I think like that?
Why do I tend to respond that way?
Why does this bother me so much?
Why can't I learn as fast as others?

Maybe labeling the problem or issue is contributing to your mind being crowded. So crowded, in fact, that you're missing the message God wants you to know.

WORRY IS A DOWN PAYMENT ON A PROBLEM YOU MAY NEVER HAVE

Answer the following question: *Is my mind too crowded?*

Is your mind crowded by worries, what-ifs, and lies?

Our minds can get so packed that a word from God has to

stand in a long line behind our own overthinking. When our minds overflow, our thought processes and logic get overwhelmed too. So, if we're being honest, whenever God tries to tell us something, our response is "Okay, God. Let me go overthink, and I'll get back to You on it."

Do you find yourself overthinking everything? Do you rehearse one what-if scenario after another? For example, when you text somebody with a question and they don't immediately answer, how do you respond? We overthink things because our minds are too crowded. A crowded mind trains the brain to traffic in suspicion: *What happens if this . . . ? What happens if they don't . . . ? What happens when . . . ?* These kinds of thoughts are rooted in either fear or a desire for control. I *fear* the outcome of this, or I want to *control* the outcome of that.

When God tells you to do something, are you ever so stuck in your own head that you talk yourself out of obedience and become paralyzed? It's not because you're under attack but because you're under a *thought*.

You are literally experiencing physical paralysis due to your mental analysis.

Overthinking is a constant loop of negative and defeated thoughts. You're not just creating a thought—you're creating a full-blown movie! It's an Oscar winner too.

Have you ever lost sleep due to the movie trailers that you create in your own head? Your emotions are the cast of characters. Your imagination crafts the scenes. And your meditations become the credits.

Remember this: Overthinking is a misuse of your creative self. Look how creative you are! You're making Oscar-worthy movies in your mind!

Here's another way to look at this: Overthinkers look into the void of uncertainty and make a forecast, and then they mentally dress for the weather conditions they have predicted.

"I'm just about to go through a storm," they say. But maybe they're not!

"I'm about to go into a wilderness," another might say. But maybe they're not!

When you overthink, you're preparing yourself, but it's not because you received a word from God or because the enemy's attacking you. It's because of your own mind—your own out-of-control thoughts. The enemy doesn't have to bother you; your mind will do that for him! He doesn't have to steal or kill anything from your life. Your mindset and your thinking are stealing and killing and destroying you through that continual repeat of negative thoughts.

Worry is a down payment on a problem you may never have.

Sometimes our minds have a death grip on the hypothetical and a loose grip on God's historical. We fail to think about what God has done; instead, we focus on what we fear might happen. But here's the truth:

The fear of the unknown or what you imagine can be greater and more debilitating than the fear of known issues or real threats.

Many of us lock on to what-if scenarios. *What if they don't like me? What if I lose my job? What if this is cancer? What if I don't get approved?* A person looking for a job might think, *What if they don't hire me?* and decide not to apply. These hypothetical worries consume and control us, moving us to make decisions based on fear, not faith. I call this a perversion of defense. It leads us to expect the worst as a defense mechanism against disappointment.

Always expecting failure or never taking opportunities so you won't be disappointed is a flawed mindset. It's true we don't experience the pain of falling from a tree if we never climb it. However, God did not create us to live at the bottom, avoiding risk and disappointment. Put another way, the miraculous doesn't happen in the boat of comfort and certainty. It's only when we step out of that boat and into the sea of uncertainty that we can walk on water.

Mystery is the workout regimen for faith. Anybody who has ever prayed "God, increase my faith" can most definitely bank on being in unpredictable situations. That's because lack of certainty deepens the roots of our faith.

If you're in ministry, uncertainty is inevitable. And if you're going to operate in any entrepreneurial endeavor, you must become comfortable with it. The Bible is full of examples where God's greatest miracles occurred in the face of the unknown. The Israelites walking toward the Red Sea with Pharaoh's army closing in must have faced immense doubt and misgivings. Yet God used that very uncertainty to showcase His power. The same can be said for the story of Nehemiah, where the people rebuilt the walls of Jerusalem each with a hammer in one hand and a sword in the other, always wondering whether they would be attacked that day. The dilemma strengthened their resolve and faith. Or consider the three young Hebrew men as they faced the fiery furnace, declaring, "God is able to deliver us. But even if He doesn't, we won't compromise." In the same way, Daniel's uncertainty must have been high as he was being led toward the lions' den.

Constant certainty will keep your faith out of shape.

Uncertainty is the workout regimen for your faith.

WHAT YOU REMEMBER WILL BE YOUR AMMUNITION OR YOUR AGGRAVATION

All throughout the fabric of Scripture, we read this word:

"Remember."

God wants us to never forget. If you battle with overthinking or if hypotheticals plague your mind, recall the following Scripture passages and *remember,* as Moses cautioned the Israelites after they spent forty years in the wilderness:

> Remember how the Lord your God led you all the way in the wilderness these forty years, to humble and test you in order to know what was in your heart, whether or not you would keep his commands. (Deuteronomy 8:2)
>
> Be careful that you do not forget the Lord your God, failing to observe his commands, his laws and his decrees that I am giving you this day. (verse 11)

The psalmist wrote, "I will remember the works of the Lord; surely I will remember Your wonders of old" (Psalm 77:11, NKJV).

After Jonah disobeyed God and ran away from Him, only to find himself sitting in stomach acid, he prayed, "When my life was ebbing away, I remembered you, Lord, and my prayer rose to you, to your holy temple" (Jonah 2:7).

The writer of Ecclesiastes reminds us: "Remember your Creator in the days of your youth, before the days of trouble come" (12:1).

During the Last Supper, Jesus told His disciples to remember: "He took bread, gave thanks and broke it, and gave it to them, saying, 'This is my body given for you; do this in remembrance of me'" (Luke 22:19).

How do you fight overthinking and worrying? You remember! You remember how far God has brought you:

I used to scroll through porn on my phone, but now I'm studying Scripture.

I stood on the street corner slinging dope, but now I'm an usher in church.

I was in jail, but now look—I'm free!

The breakup of that relationship was so painful! But God has helped me see that it wasn't His best for me.

I remember the fear and worry about whether I had enough to pay the next month's rent. But God provided.

We also must never forget to give God our "I remember" prayers of gratitude:

"I remember where I was before You found me, Lord."

"I remember how You've shown me Your holiness and Your might in my life."

Keep this in mind: What you remember will be your ammunition or your aggravation!

OUR EYES, MINDS, AND HEARTS ARE NOT FRIENDS

The only things you can control in the healing process are your effort and your attitude.

We need to understand that many times, our eyes, minds, and hearts are not friends. Nor are they romantically involved. Something we need to do—something I still deal with myself—is to constantly battle to think on the promises and the faithfulness of God even when our eyes are telling us to believe something else.

I have to keep telling my eyes, "Don't believe that! Don't believe what you see!" That's because we walk by faith and not by sight. I must remind myself to believe not in what I'm seeing but in the Word of God that I have in my heart. I need to daily meditate on God's Word.

A transformed life requires mind renewal. As Romans 12:2 says, "Do not conform to the pattern of this world, but be transformed by the renewing of your mind. Then you will be able to test and approve what God's will is—his good, pleasing and perfect will." If you want a transformed life, you have to renew your mind. If you want transformed peace and joy, you have to renew your mind so that you can test and discern God's good, pleasing, and perfect will.

When my mind is renewed, I can test every thought accurately.

Renewing the mind is a process that requires intentionality, prayer, and discipline. This reminds me of when I called out to Jesus to detox me from all the filth I had put before my eyes. It's a prayer I'm praying over you.

"God, heal my mind. Heal it from the harmful content I've consumed, from the thoughts that have polluted it, from the lies I've believed. Heal the way I think, what I concentrate on, and what I reason. Because healing the mind is the foundation of everything."

Healing your mind requires clearing the clutter inside it. To do that, you must understand how your mind can be so crowded and how the enemy's lies can become so crushing. Some of us can't distinguish what God's hand is on simply because our minds are so unhealthy. You can't recognize whether God is endorsing something if your mind has not been renewed.

Again, a transformed life is tied to mind renewal. You can attend church your whole life and never be transformed. You can sing worship songs and never be transformed. The reason is that you're not allowing the Word of God to renew and wash your mind. A healed mind thinks differently. A renewed mind causes you to speak and hear differently.

How do we fight to renew our minds? As long as I've been in church, I've heard so many sermons telling me to renew my mind. My question has always been "How?" So, I'm going to share some of my methodologies for keeping my mind focused on the promises and the goodness of God, even when my eyes tell me to believe something else.

THE MIND IS LIKE SOIL

We first must begin to view our minds as soil. Picture your mind as fertile ground that produces whatever is planted in it. The conversations you have, the media you consume, the music you listen to—all of these are seeds. What you allow into your mind shapes what grows in your life. These seeds might be good or bad things, depending on the process of mind renewal you are currently engaged in.

For example, you may think clearing your browser history wipes away evidence of the harmful sites you visit, but even though they're deleted from the device, those seeds remain in your mind. That favorite TV show you watch every day? Seed. The music that fills your ears? Seed. The conversation you had with a friend via text? Seed. The social media you scroll through? Seed.

Are those seeds serving you in this season of your life? Are they contributing to your growth, or are they unhealthy for your faith?

Here's the thing: Soil doesn't care what type of seed it holds. It can be a seed of positivity, negativity, truth, or lies. Soil's only job is to nurture the seed and push the seed's identity out into the world. So, if your life is filled with confusion, chaos, or toxicity, it's a reflection of the seeds that have been planted and nurtured in the soil of your mind.

Once you understand that your mind is soil, the next step is to become intentional about who and what you allow into your mental garden. Healing your mind takes work. Once you've done the work to uproot unhealthy patterns and beliefs, you'll naturally become more selective about who speaks into your life and what you expose yourself to. This isn't about being rude or closed off; it's about guarding your heart with diligence, because your mind controls the flow of your life.

A healed mind doesn't allow just anyone or anything to plant seeds. The hard work it takes to detox the mind and heal unhealthy thought patterns means you must be vigilant. Whether it's relationships, conversations, or media, what you let in matters. Every conversation, song, and show you engage with is a seed.

What will you allow to grow in your life? Guard your mind, protect your garden, and plant seeds that align with God's truth and purpose for you.

WHAT THE DEVIL WANTS MOST IS YOUR MIND

Our minds get cluttered by thoughts we create on our own and by seeds planted by other people or things in our lives. But some thoughts that are in your head are not your own. They are Satan-induced ponderings. Some thoughts are seeds planted by the enemy, designed to take root in your mind and grow into actions that lead you away from God's purpose for your life.

Satan loves to plant thoughts in the form of doubt, fear, and deception. These seeds, if watered, will grow into full-fledged actions. The way you water a thought is by speaking it and acting on it.

Consider Jesus's interaction with Peter in Mark 8:32–33. Jesus plainly told His disciples about His upcoming death and resurrection, but Peter rebuked Him. Jesus responded, "Get behind me, Satan! . . . You do not have in mind the concerns of God but merely human concerns." Peter's thoughts weren't his own— they were planted by the enemy, because Satan knew that Jesus's death would fulfill God's plan.

What is the enemy truly after? What he wants most is your mind. He loves to plant seeds of doubt, despair, and disappointment because those seeds can bear devastating fruit if watered.

How do we water them? By meditating on them. We can always tell whether a thought seed has matured into a crop by our words. Let me show you an example of this from the Bible.

At the opening of the book of Job, Satan is having a conversation with the Lord:

> "Does Job fear God for nothing?" Satan replied. "Have you not put a hedge around him and his household and everything he has? You have blessed the work of his hands, so that his flocks and herds are spread throughout the land. But now stretch out your hand and strike everything he has, and he will surely curse you to your face." (1:9–11)

After Job is heavily afflicted by pain and loss and death and tragedy, he still doesn't curse God, so Satan tries something else. When the enemy can't get to you, he will try to influence those who can. So, who could influence Job the most? His wife. "His wife said to him, 'Are you still maintaining your integrity? Curse God and die!'" (2:9).

This is the same thing Satan had said Job would do if he was afflicted (1:11). Obviously, the enemy gave Job's wife that thought. This is proof that some thoughts aren't yours but Satan-induced ponderings! The devil gave Job's wife this seed of a thought, and she meditated on it and watered it. Eventually it went from seed to maturity, and she uttered it.

Satan doesn't want you to fulfill your purpose. That is why he will plant seeds of doubt, fear, and confusion, hoping they'll take root and grow. You must understand that your mind is a battlefield so you can perceive when a thought isn't aligned with God's will. With discernment and maturity, you can recognize these lies, take every thought captive, and choose to plant seeds of truth instead.

CORTISOL AND DOPAMINE WILL NEVER GO ON A DATE

How can you keep your mind from becoming so cluttered and crowded that a word from God can't get in?

Remember who your Father is

I covered this earlier in the chapter, but I'll remind you again: Interwoven throughout the fabric of Scripture is a constant tone of encouragement to remember God. For example, Deuteronomy 8:18 says, "Remember the LORD your God, for it is he who gives you the ability to produce wealth, and so confirms his covenant, which he swore to your ancestors, as it is today."

So, your ability to produce wealth comes from where? It's not how hard you grind or how naturally gifted you are. It won't come from the PhD you earned. It is God who gives you the ability.

All throughout the Bible, we are reminded to remember our Father. Remember your Daddy. Why? Because *remember* has two definitions. The first is "to bring back to mind or think of again."[1] It means to recall or bookmark an experience. The second definition is "to reconstitute or reassemble"[2] —to put back together (as in, re-member). The enemy wants you to remember your trauma to dismember your joy, peace, and confidence. He wants you to remember the pain of what you went through to dismember your peace of mind. That is why God wants you to remember Him. He wants to put back together the joy and confidence that you've lost.

1. *Merriam-Webster Dictionary,* "remember," merriam-webster.com/dictionary /remember.
2. Wiktionary, "re-member," last edited August 19, 2024, 04:37, en.wiktionary.org /wiki/re-member#English.

As I said, what you remember is either your ammunition or your aggravation. It is the ammunition that clears the line of overthinking or the aggravation that keeps that crowded line long. The enemy is a terrorist of the mind. This is what he attacks.

So, how do you start the process of removing the clutter from your mind? Remember who your Father is.

Remember to meditate on God's Word

Psalm 1:2 says, "His delight is in the law of the LORD; and in His law he meditates day and night" (NKJV). Here the psalmist is telling us how to remove the crowds in our minds. It's tied to our devotional lives—we are commanded to meditate on the Word day and night. Doing this is an investment in our joy currency, because what we remember will serve as either our ammunition or our aggravation. And this has neurological implications.

Memories are like bookmarks that bring you back to various experiences. Remembering a positive event causes your brain to release dopamine, the neurotransmitter we label as the reward chemical.[3] This dopamine is your ammunition. But a chemical release happens in the opposite direction too. Constantly meditating on and rehearsing a terrible memory causes your brain to release cortisol—the body's stress hormone.[4]

Here's the problem: Your reward chemical and your stress chemical cannot function simultaneously. They cannot be at equal levels at the same time. One will outweigh the other. So,

3. Amy Novotney, "Feeling Nostalgic This Holiday Season? It Might Help Boost Your Mental Health," American Psychological Association, December 18, 2023, apa.org /topics/mental-health/nostalgia-boosts-well-being.

4. Ruhr-Universitaet-Bochum, "How the stress hormone cortisol reinforces traumatic memories," ScienceDaily, July 1, 2015, sciencedaily.com/releases/2015/07 /150701083336.htm.

what I meditate on will either release dopamine or release cortisol.

We need to do what Philippians 4:8 urges us to do: "Finally,
brothers and sisters, whatever is true, whatever is noble, whatever is right, whatever is pure, whatever is lovely, whatever is
admirable—if anything is excellent or praiseworthy—think about
such things."

Breathe and remember

When the Scripture tells us to be still, God is telling us to breathe.
Right now as you're reading this, I want you to do a simple exer-
cise. Just breathe in through your nose and out through your
mouth.

Breathe, God tells us. That lowers cortisol levels.

As you inhale through your nose and exhale through your
mouth, slowly and steadily, I want you to hear God saying this:

Breathe and relax. I've got you.
I'm not going to let you drown.
I'm a good father.
I'm never going to leave you. I'm never going to forsake you.
Breathe and inhale My promises and what I've told you about Myself.
Exhale everything that's not true.

Yes, you messed up, but you're not a mistake. Your mess-ups have
been hung up (Colossians 2:14). *So, breathe and relax.*

Always remember the reason God allows us to go through trials:

Remember how I got you through the last time?
Remember how I got you the job when nobody else was hiring?
Remember how I helped you heal from that divorce?

Remember how I made a way out of no way?

Remember how I caught your tears and helped your mind get restored?

The only reason that you still have your sanity and haven't lost your mind is because I was there.

Remember who your God is and what He has said about you. Then breathe and keep on remembering that.

Remember God's truths and forget the lies

I'll say this again: When you begin to overthink, ask yourself, *Who put that thought in my mind?* Can't think of a name? It's either you or the enemy. Recall the story of Job and those Satan-induced ponderings.

"Are you still maintaining your integrity?" Job's wife asked him. "Curse God and die!"

We must always remember what God has told us versus the lies our minds are telling us.

Remember to not believe everything you think

Our thoughts are not always facts. So, don't believe everything you think, because every thought is not yours.

Surely every thought going through your head is not true. You must filter your automatic thoughts through your core beliefs. This is a good time to pause and jot down some of your core beliefs and how they are empowering or hindering you. One of my core beliefs that has proved powerful is this: God is faithful, and He has provided for me. That's the filter I use with any automatic thought. My core belief helps me overcome any thought that says otherwise.

So, how do you get the Word of God to no longer stand in the back of the long line of your crowded thoughts and overthinking? You have to know who your Father is. Meditate on His Word and what He said about you. Breathe. Then ask yourself who your thoughts are coming from. And never believe everything you think.

PROBLEMS ARE INVITATIONS FOR THE MIRACULOUS

As I write this, our local church has been experiencing massive growth. Throughout this process, I've been asking and seeking God for a larger gathering place. On one particular blessed Sunday, as I noticed people walking down the street and being shuttled back and forth to our church, I couldn't help asking God when He was going to give us a bigger building. The buses weren't moving fast enough to get people from the parking lot to the building, and all our overflows were filled.

"When is it going to happen, Lord?"

But as I looked outside, I saw our church's TRY ME flag blowing in the wind, and it reminded me of what God told me in November 2019:

Try Me, Jerry.

Little did I know then how timely this instruction would turn out to be.

At the time, my mom and dad had just told me they wanted me to be the lead pastor, but I had said no. Being the lead pastor at that time meant I had to lead service on Thursday nights, while Sunday mornings were reserved for the senior pastor. And nobody held church services on weekdays anymore. But while I was at the church vacuuming, I felt like I heard God telling me, *Try Me.* So, I told my wife, Tanisha, what happened.

"You know, they're talking about making me lead pastor. I had this funny feeling I heard God saying, *Try Me.* But I don't know."

"So, try Him," Tanisha told me.

I agreed to do it, and we started in January 2020. Two months later, the pandemic hit and shut everything down. Now I was mad.

I told You this would happen. Why now?

But that's exactly when our ministry took off. Everybody was in quarantine; we couldn't have more than ten people total in our church. So, it was just me with the audio, video, and visual streaming team—and *boom* . . . everything blew up.

Through that experience, I learned something that I like to share with others:

You have to remember that God is in your tomorrow *today.*
You see the corner, but He sees around it.

That was why God spoke *Try Me* to my heart. I tried Him, and my life has never been the same.

Back to the present day. On that morning as I saw the flag and looked at all the people coming to hear the Word of the Lord— not to hear me but to hear from God—my dad told me something:

"God is setting something up," he said. "God likes doing this."

Remember, God likes to get us right next to the Red Sea where the mist is hitting our faces. God likes to get us in the fiery furnace so we can see the fourth man in the fire. God likes to get us close enough to smell the odor of the lions' den. He wants to get us right up there before He steps in to help.

I needed that moment to remind me. I needed to look back and remember.

Remember, Jerry, God told me. *I hear you now just like I heard you back in November 2019. And I'll tell you the same thing: Try Me. You don't think that I see this church? These are My people. You don't think that I care about My children? I'm going to handle it. You just follow Me.*

In very real time I was experiencing what it looks like to remove the crowd from your mind. I had to remember what my Heavenly Father said and who He is.

God doesn't want to stand in a long line of clutter filling your mind. His Word won't be heard in a mind full of fear, worry, doubt, failure, insecurity, malice, and pain. Remove those things from your mind so that the Word can have unlimited access to your heart!

QUESTIONS

1. What voices are the loudest in your mind right now? Which of these voices do you need to turn down so you can hear God more clearly?
2. How often do you find yourself catastrophizing or creating worst-case scenarios? What truths from God's Word can help combat these thoughts?
3. What specific memories can you focus on to release dopamine instead of cortisol? How can you practice remembering God's faithfulness to you?
4. In what practical ways can you create more space in your mind for God's voice? What daily habits might help declutter your thoughts?

PRAYER

God, declutter my mind. I want Your thoughts, Your Word, and Your peace to have unlimited access to my heart and spirit. Please help me remove the crowd of thoughts that keep me from hearing Your Word. Help me remember Your promises, Your faithfulness, and Your goodness over the terror of the mental scenarios I create in my head. Forgive me for every time I delayed obedience because I had to think about it first and get back to You. Heal me in my mind, because I want to be transformed. And I recognize through scriptures like Romans 12:2 that transformation is married to a renewed mind. Renew my mind, Lord. Declutter my mind. In Jesus's name, amen.

BONUS CONTENT

To continue rehabbing your heart, use your smartphone to scan the code for a bonus video diving deeper into the content of this chapter.

URL: waterbrookmultnomah.com/HRChapterFour

FIVE

WHAT'S THE WORST THAT COULD HAPPEN?

Moses answered, "What if they do not believe me or listen to me and say, 'The LORD did not appear to you'?"

—EXODUS 4:1

When I was seven years old, we moved into a house that had a pool in the backyard. You can just imagine my excitement. My mom, however, didn't quite share my enthusiasm.

"This is what we have to do," Mom told my dad. "If this is going to be the house that we own, we've got to teach our son how to swim."

LIFE JACKETS ARE MADE FOR TRAINING, NOT LIVING

So, that's exactly what my father did for the next month and a half. Every day, he would put a life jacket on me, we would go into the backyard, and I'd swim. Each time I got into the shallow side of the pool, I felt more confident in the water. My dad taught me things like how to backstroke and hold my breath underwater. Then one day as we reached the edge of the pool, my father lost his mind.

"All right," he said, "take off the life jacket and jump in."

At first I thought I had heard wrong. The pool was twelve feet in the deep end. I had jumped off the diving board before, but I always had my life jacket on.

"So, you want me to commit suicide?" I asked him. "You want to go to jail for murder? I'm not taking off my life jacket!"

"Don't worry," my father told me. "If you go under, Daddy's gonna jump in and save you."

I refused. "Nope. No way."

For a while we went back and forth as he tried to encourage me and I adamantly refused. The truth was, I had more faith in my life jacket than in my father. I was fearing the worst possible outcome: drowning. But I conjured up that fear in my own head.

This is what can happen when you expect the worst.

I'm not taking off my life jacket, because I already know how this is going to go. I'm going to jump in and go under, and you're going to try and save me. But I'll go down faster than you can swim, and I'm going to die!

I had played out the entire scene in my mind, so I told myself I wasn't going to do it.

How many of us have this same type of mentality with our faith? Do you have a life-jacket Christianity? You know—the casual Christianity where you like to play it safe? The kind where you tell yourself you can't do what God asks you to do because you might drown? You expect the worst and ask yourself all sorts of questions.

Maybe that's the problem. We're having conversations with ourselves more than listening to the conversation of the Holy Spirit.

Does fearing the worst thing that can happen make you cling to the life jacket of safe Christianity instead of experiencing a twelve-foot-deep blessing? Do you ever argue with your Heavenly Father and remain content to settle for the shallow water?

What depths of life is God calling you to jump into but you're determined to stay in the shallow end?

What ocean does God want you to dive into but you're comfortable drifting in a pond?

What reservoir does God have for you to experience but you're more than happy with a simple cup?

I will never forget what my father told me that day:

"Life jackets are made for training, not living."

I love that line.

How many times do we cling to training wheels when God wants to give us an automobile? Another mode of transportation will get us to our destination faster, but since we expect the worst and fear the new method, we continue to embrace those training wheels.

For so many of us, one of the worst places we can live is in our heads, because our minds constantly meditate on the worst-case scenarios. Maybe your mind dwells on and ponders the worst possible outcome for any situation. You predict the disappointment and defeat, so you prepare for it. You mentally wade in an ocean of failure before you even jump into the water. Does this sound familiar?

In the previous chapter, we covered how the mind can become crowded and cluttered. Now I want to dive a little deeper into how our minds are often plagued by thinking the worst. Our negative thinking can become a psychological terrorist holding our lives hostage. All too often, we expect a bad outcome from an action we haven't even started. Recurring and incessant projections become precursors to everything we do.

This isn't going to work.
I know they won't like my idea.

He's going to say no.
They won't hire me.
I can't finish that.
What if I fail?

So many times, we expect the worst. We fear failure, and we remain content with our life-jacket Christianity.

What would you do if there was no such thing as a worst-case scenario? What would happen if you took off the life jacket suffocating your potential and jumped into the waters of possibility? What gift would you give birth to? What book would you write? What song would you sing? What act of obedience would not be delayed? Who could be forgiven? What ministry idea or podcast or entrepreneurial pursuit would you give birth to if a worst-case scenario didn't exist?

In this chapter, I want you to see how fear operates. Negative thinking is the role you play in your own suffering. It stops you from reaching the you that God created you to be. Creating worst-case scenarios keeps your blessings stuck. We must learn to trust that God has a plan for us.

WE'VE BEEN MISLABELING DIFFICULTY
AS IMPOSSIBILITY

There are three destiny-crippling words that I began to hear in my early childhood and then heard among my fellow students in college and among my neighbors in my community. I've even heard this statement among believers. These three words can destroy your destiny:

I fear failure.

Do you ever feel like that? How many times have you thought this?

The truth is, many times the fear of failure is worse than failure itself. Too often, our fearful perspectives, outlooks, and mentalities about outcomes are worse than our failings. Because here's the thing: Failure is not defeat. It is not even fatal. Quitting is.

Did you get that?

Failure isn't fatal, but quitting is. Quitting on the things that God wants us to complete is getting in the way of our experiencing peace.

You don't get growth without failure. For instance, many bodybuilders and people who are passionate about fitness will push themselves toward muscle failure because this positions them to build larger muscles. Without a level of discomfort, strain, regimen, and soreness, there will be muscles I won't grow and develop. Being an effective bodybuilder requires pushing your body to the point of failure.

What if I told you that the greatest risk is to not even take one?

We also need to consider the flip side of failure: Sometimes failure is succeeding the most in what matters the least. If I get the cars and the possessions, if I build the platform, if I achieve the power and status and notoriety yet do not do what I was born to do, then I've failed. Many times, what the culture considers successful, the kingdom of God considers failure.

What does success look like? I challenge you to accurately and appropriately define success—not based on your own standards but backed up with Scripture. Find at least four or five passages in the Bible that support your definition and demonstrate that it is in line with God's heart. If you can't find that many passages to back up your definition of success, you need to revise it. However, I do want to encourage you to make it personal. What I consider successful might be a failure for you. What's successful for you might be a failure for me because I'm not supposed to do what you are. I'm to do only what God has called me to do. This is why comparison is so dangerous.

What is my definition of success?

I need to occupy each and every room that God ordained for me to occupy while I'm here for His glory. I need to complete and fulfill the reason I have been born.

Are there rooms you're not stepping in to occupy because you fear failure? Are you not fulfilling the reason you have been born because you fear the worst that can happen?

Here's something I've noticed: We often mislabel anything that's difficult as impossible. We think to ourselves, *Nobody can do that*, but in reality, it's just difficult. It will be hard and will force us to practice more and to get up earlier. It'll require us to be more excellent with our gifts, our business, and our verbiage—but it's not *impossible*. Don't mislabel difficulty as impossibility!

Stop surrendering your mind and your outlook to terror.

So many of us cannot move because of fear.

We need to remember the Israelites in the wilderness when Moses was talking to them about Canaan, the Promised Land:

> Taking with them some of the fruit of the land, [the twelve spies] brought it down to us and reported, "It is a good land that the Lord our God is giving us." But you were unwilling to go up; you rebelled against the command of the Lord your God. You grumbled in your tents and said, "The Lord hates us; so he brought us out of Egypt to deliver us into the hands of the Amorites to destroy us. Where can we go? Our brothers have made our hearts melt in fear." . . . You did not trust in the Lord your God, who went ahead of you on your journey. (Deuteronomy 1:25–28, 32–33)

The Israelites' fears wouldn't allow them to obey God. Their terrors wouldn't allow them to trust God. That's why they had to stay in the wilderness for forty years. They couldn't move on because of their fears. They feared the worst.

So many times, we fear the same thing—an outcome we can't control. But God wants to remind all of us that He did not give us the spirit of fear.

Have you allowed fear to become your therapist? Do you have to book a session with it before you obey God?

God didn't give you that spirit.

The outcome, the results, the impact, belong to God.

Tomorrow belongs to God.

So, maybe you fear failure because you're afraid God will direct your steps in a way you don't desire. As Proverbs 16:9 says, "We can make our plans, but the LORD determines our steps" (NLT). Do you call something a failure when it was really the Lord? Proverbs 20:24 states, "The LORD directs our steps, so why try to understand everything along the way?" (NLT).

God is running this. So, why do we constantly try to figure out what's going to happen and how something will be? You will torment yourself trying to be God!

Do you doubt that the Lord cares about the details of your life? Study Exodus 25–31, and recognize how detailed He wanted His people to build His tabernacle. God cared about *every* intricate part of that building. So, what makes you think He doesn't care about every detail of your life? Look at Psalm 37:23–24: "The LORD directs the steps of the godly. He delights in every detail of their lives. Though they stumble, they will never fall, for the LORD holds them by the hand" (NLT).

The fear of failure asks, "God, will You really hold me? God, will You really be with me? God, do You really care about every detail? Because if You do, then why haven't You done anything yet?"

God says He will hold your hand. But the fear of failure is asking God whether this is really true or telling Him you don't like the steps He is directing because they aren't going the way you planned.

That's basically telling God, "I want Your will my way."

We need to remember to pray this way:

"Dear God, give me the strength to no longer allow fear to have the final say. Help me know that my steps are ordered."

God is the one directing our steps. Yes, we might stumble, but we will never fall, because the Lord is holding us by His hand.

THROUGH THE EYES OF OUR HEARTS WE SEE GOD'S HOPE

We need to be trained to see situations through the eyes of our hearts, not just the eyes on our heads. The eyes of your face give you sight, but the eyes of your heart give you *insight*.

In Ephesians 1:18, Paul writes, "I pray that the eyes of your heart may be enlightened in order that you may know the hope to which he has called you, the riches of his glorious inheritance in his holy people." He's not talking about the eyes of your head or the eyes of your perspective. He is praying that the eyes of your heart may be enlightened. Why? So you may know the hope to which God has called you.

When we dwell on the worst-case scenario, we think without hope, which is a perversion of hope. To ponder the worst-case scenario is to think without faith, which is a perversion of faith. It's having faith that the worst outcome is going to happen, that the situation won't work in your favor for God's glory. It's having faith that the whole thing will fail. This is a perversion of faith—it is faith in reverse.

Paul tells us that he wants the eyes of our hearts to be enlightened so that we may have hope. Looking only with the eyes on your head can rob you of hope. But when you open the eyes of your heart, you can see beyond what's visible—you can have insight.

There is a difference between sight and insight. Let me explain. Sight means gazing at the exterior. Insight, however, means glancing at the exterior but gazing at the interior. Think about this: A gaze is a fixed stare. I can fix my stare on the economy. I can stare at the latest horrific news or at gas prices. I can stare at my shortcomings. Sight is to have a fixed stare on the exterior. But insight is to glance at all these things—to just take a brief look at the exterior—and then to gaze at the interior.

Here's another difference between sight and insight: Sight focuses on what is seen, while insight is the knowledge, understanding, and revelation of the unseen. So, the reason we keep having the worst-case scenario many times is because we see the situation as being catastrophic. Proverbs 23:7 says, "As he thinketh in his heart, so is he" (KJV). Seeing bleeds over into our thinking. What we think affects what we see: "We walk by faith, not by sight" (2 Corinthians 5:7, KJV).

We need to train ourselves to see with the eyes of our hearts. When we see with the eyes of our hearts, we remember the hope God has called us to.

DISAPPOINTMENT CAN BE DIRECTION
INSTEAD OF DEVASTATION

Let me introduce you to a word you might not be familiar with: *Catastrophizing.*

This is a term used in therapy and psychology to describe the pattern of dwelling on and expecting worst-case scenarios. Catastrophizing involves believing that you are in a worse situation

than you really are or that the worst possible outcome is imminent.[1] Some who catastrophize not only are convinced that the
most catastrophic thing will happen but also might prepare and
plan for it.

Many people who engage in catastrophizing are exhausted.
This treadmill of negative thinking wears you out by keeping you
in the same place. When you run on a treadmill, you're not going
anywhere, yet you sweat and breathe hard and grind, and your
heart rate stays up. This is what catastrophizing does—it causes
you to live a treadmill life, always exhausted but stuck in the same
place with the same attitude. So, year after year, you run yourself
to death with the same perspective. The same issue. Same time.
Same outcome. Same fatigue.

Then what happens? This debilitating weariness spawns addiction. As soon as you wake up, you think, *I gotta have my coffee. I
can't work without my coffee!* Then it becomes *I can't do this without
my pills!* It's a cover-up that you are exhausted and are scrambling
to find something to treat that exhaustion. *Gotta have my weed.
Gotta have sex. Gotta have my false escape.* Why? Because you are so
tired of your own mind. You are trying to find some way to escape your thoughts. You are trying to get some sleep, some peace.
And in the background, the Holy Spirit is there wanting to give
you that sleep and peace. But as we discovered in the last chapter,
the Holy Spirit is stuck at the back of a long line and can't get in.

Are you exhausted because you're using all your gas to fear
and dwell on things that don't matter for your destiny? That's catastrophizing.

Our culture has us labeling as impossible anything that's different or difficult, and this can often lead us to catastrophizing. Let
me give you an example that happened in our family recently.

1. Jenna Fletcher, "What Is Catastrophizing?" PsychCentral, updated April 22, 2022,
psychcentral.com / lib / what-is-catastrophizing.

Our son Josiah is a few months away from turning two. The doctor says he's not talking as much as he should. At his age, he should be able to say around fifty words, but Josiah is saying only words like "Mama" and "Da-da" and his sister's name.

"What if he doesn't talk?" Tanisha asked me. "What if he has a speech impediment?"

I reminded her that the same thing happened with our first-born son, Jerry III.

"We had this with J," I said. "He's going to talk. And when he does, you're going to be like, 'Man, he talks too much!'"

I am not suggesting that if we have enough faith God will always spare us or those we love from difficulty or suffering. But I am saying that trusting God means refusing to always assume the worst. Your perspective is shaped by the algorithm in your mind. Think of this similarly to how social media works. Whatever you search for the most will show up in your feed. If you look up basketball a lot, it's going to pop up on your suggested feeds. Maybe it's cooking or art. Whatever it might be, it will turn up in your feed because the algorithm is cultivated by your search. Your mind is the same way. Your perspective is cultivated by the algorithm of your thoughts. So, whatever you think about the most is going to shape your perspective.

This is why the Scriptures tell us to meditate on the Word of the Lord. Meditate on His decrees day and night. Why? Because your perspective will be shaped by the algorithm of your thoughts.

Again, Proverbs 23:7 says, "As he thinketh in his heart, so is he" (KJV).

Thoughts can become projections. This is how negative people project on you. A person who has a negative thought about themselves can project it on you or on something you're about to do. Deep down they feel that if they were to do it, the worst possible outcome would happen. So, they share their negativity with you: "I wouldn't do that because . . ." The real reason they wouldn't do it is that they operate only in catastrophizing.

Many people do this. After parents say something in anger, they may believe their children will never talk to them again. If a professor makes an inaccurate statement, he might be convinced that his students will never respect him again. A co-worker who messes up a presentation might think she'll never be invited to work on a project again. People in these situations may warn you of outcomes that they fear for themselves. The "advice" they give you is simply a projection of their negative thoughts.

How does a person develop a pattern of catastrophizing? I want to highlight a few ways.

THE PARANOIA OF REPEATED PAIN

We often think worst-case-scenario thoughts when we experience pain from a loved one and then tell somebody all the hurtful things that happened to us, only to have them hurt us in the same way. Once this takes place, it's so easy to always expect the worst, to assume that this will happen again. You fear having that pain again, so you stop being open and vulnerable. You continually assume something bad will happen because it did before, and it hurt even worse the second time around.

Many times, negative thinking is the punishment you give yourself because somebody else couldn't keep their word. So, this makes you decide to not open up and talk to a person, even though God may have placed them in your life to help you heal. Yes, the enemy sends people, but so does God.

The enemy can send a Delilah, but God can send a Paul.

The enemy might use a Pharaoh, but God can use a Naomi.

God uses people to get us to places we need to be. But if you never trust another person to take you there, you will be stuck in the same spot for the rest of your life.

Did somebody break your heart? Does that mean you're never going to open your heart to love again?

This is why healing is so important. When someone hurts you or doesn't keep their word, your negative thinking can cause you to punish yourself. So, you start catastrophizing and hiding the real you. You hide the part of you your mother or father didn't know how to parent. Or you hide the part of you your pastor didn't shepherd.

We can all hide parts of ourselves because of the pain we've experienced—not only from a loved one but also from someone we shared that pain with who then hurt us in the same way.

LOOPED DISAPPOINTMENTS

The second reason I believe a lot of people default to worst-case scenarios is because of looped disappointments. Since this and that and the other thing didn't work, they're preparing themselves to be disappointed again. We assume disappointment plays on loop.

But what if we learned to view disappointment as direction versus devastation?

Before my wife met me, she was in a relationship with somebody who cheated on her. That pain she experienced was disappointing, but a year later when I came to the church, God was showing her that her former boyfriend was not her future husband. He was not her opportunity and not the person God had designed for her. Yes, she was disappointed, but she didn't allow that disappointment to devastate her.

What sort of disappointment have you received recently? Do you believe it is meant to direct you and not devastate you? Maybe it's God sending you a necessary message:

That's not where your favor is.

It's not time.

That's not the person you're meant to be with.

That's not the job you're meant to work in.

Are you crying over something that God doesn't have for you in your life?

Are you frustrated with God because He won't bless something that's not His will?

Is your soul so downcast because you want something that will ultimately sabotage your relationship with God?

Maybe this is not for devastation but for direction.

When we have that perspective, we can withstand everything in our lives that doesn't go the way we want it to, because we know God has something better for us. This must not be God's timing right now.

Maybe your plan was for *your* glory. It was just for *you*. And maybe that wouldn't have made God look good. Maybe it wouldn't have shown off His grace and mercy. Maybe it would have simply increased your following, not His.

In John 14:1–3, Jesus said:

> Let not your heart be troubled; you believe in God, believe also in Me. In My Father's house are many mansions; if it were not so, I would have told you. I go to prepare a place for you. And if I go and prepare a place for you, I will come again and receive you to Myself; that where I am, there you may be also. (NKJV)

Jesus is reminding us that He is "the way, the truth, and the life" (verse 6). Jesus is preparing a place for us. He is telling us He has something better prepared, so we shouldn't let our hearts be troubled.

Don't be devastated by that disappointment you're currently experiencing. Don't let those disappointments become endless loops that keep your life locked down.

A PERVERSION OF DEFENSE

The third reason people catastrophize is that this is a perversion of defense. Expecting the worst is often a defense mechanism against disappointment. In other words, if I think the worst is going to happen, I am less likely to be disappointed. I want to defend my heart from getting hurt, so I'm going to assume things won't work out.

Do you ever find yourself playing it safe in life to avoid getting hurt?

I'm going to play it safe because I can't feel the pain of a fall if I don't climb.

I won't feel the pain of being rejected if I don't post my thoughts.

I won't feel the pain of breaking up if I don't voice my standards.

Do you avoid taking action so you won't have to experience what disappointment feels like? This is trafficking in negative thoughts. This is a perversion of defense that leads to catastrophizing.

IT'S DIFFICULT TO HEAR DUE TO THE STATIC OF YOUR THOUGHTS

Do you want to see one of the best examples of someone who had a severe case of catastrophizing? Let's look at Moses, one of my favorite icons.

Exodus 2:23–25 sets the stage:

> During that long period, the king of Egypt died. The
> Israelites groaned in their slavery and cried out, and
> their cry for help because of their slavery went up to
> God. God heard their groaning and he remembered
> his covenant with Abraham, with Isaac and with
> Jacob. So God looked on the Israelites and was con-
> cerned about them.

In Exodus 3, God comes to Moses with a work for him to do. God intended Moses to be a package for His glory. There are people praying to God, so He is going to answer them by sending Moses. God wants to show His goodness through Moses, so He gives Moses a command: "Now, go. I am sending you to Pharaoh to bring my people the Israelites out of Egypt" (verse 10).

Right away Moses starts thinking about the worst-case scenario and making excuses to God. "Who am I to do something like that?" he asks.

God reassures Moses that He will be with him and answers his question about who Moses should say sent him. But at the start of Exodus 4, Moses is still thinking the worst:

> Moses answered, "What if they do not believe me or
> listen to me and say, 'The LORD did not appear to
> you'?"
>
> Then the LORD said to him, "What is that in your
> hand?"
>
> "A staff," he replied.
>
> The LORD said, "Throw it on the ground."
>
> Moses threw it on the ground and it became a
> snake, and he ran from it. (verses 1–3)

Consider this: God wasn't going to make a snake only to cause it to bite and kill Moses. Yet Moses runs from it, thinking the worst.

God gives Moses more signs to show the Israelites in case they don't believe him. After Moses's staff turns into a snake, his hand becomes leprous—"white as snow" (verse 6)—when he puts it in his cloak. If those two signs don't work, God tells Moses, then "take some water from the Nile" and it will "become blood on the ground" (verse 9).

Moses, however, continues to catastrophize:

> Moses said to the LORD, "Pardon your servant, Lord. I have never been eloquent, neither in the past nor since you have spoken to your servant. I am slow of speech and tongue." (verse 10)

Moses assumes that he's going to be the world's worst communicator, that he's the worst person in the world to deliver a message like this to Pharaoh. But God reminds Moses who gave human beings their ability to talk, promising that He will be with him. But once again, Moses remains doubtful: "Pardon your servant, Lord. Please send someone else" (verse 13).

Why is Moses having this back-and-forth conversation with God? He is stuck expecting the worst-case scenario, and he's thinking only about himself. He is engaged in catastrophizing, convincing himself this is not going to work. As a result, his mind is stuck on a loop, asking every what-if question he can think of.

Do you ever find yourself thinking of so many worst possible outcomes that you end up getting in the way of people you have been summoned to help? Maybe your catastrophizing is preventing you from loving your children the way they need to be loved. Maybe your worst-case scenario is stopping you from sharing the message that will help someone break an addiction. Perhaps all your what-ifs are keeping you from blessing others and being used by God in a mighty way.

When God comes to Moses and tells him to go to Pharaoh to

bring His people out of Egypt, He is talking to the answer. The answer is Moses. But Moses is thinking about worst-case scenarios. Do you ever do the same?

While we're doubting our gift or not being obedient, somebody is in bondage.

While we're stuck because we're terrified of what could happen, somebody is in bondage.

Somebody right now is praying to God, and you are an answer! But you can't deliver that answer if you constantly let worst-case scenarios talk you out of what God is talking you into.

Is your negative thinking interfering with your ability to hear your Shepherd? Look at John 10:27: "My sheep listen to my voice; I know them, and they follow me." It's difficult to hear God when something louder than Him is playing in your mind.

If you can stop the static by quitting the worst-case-scenario rehearsal, you can begin to hear your Shepherd clearly. Your deliverance from catastrophic thinking might be for somebody else's freedom, where the glory of the Lord can be displayed not for you but for them.

REST IN THE PROMISES, NOT THE PARANOIA

So, how do we get over thinking the worst? How do we keep our minds from catastrophizing? Here are a few ways:

Rest in the promises of God, not the paranoia.

Rest in the fact that God is not going to let you drown.

Rest in the fact that heaven doesn't have a shortage.

Rest in the fact that all things work together and that, in due season, a harvest will come.

Rest in the fact that God is preparing a place for you.

Rest in the fact that God is behind the scenes, on the scene, and before the scenes. He was there before you even thought of having a scene!

We need to rest in all of these and not in paranoia.

When did God provide Adam with Eve? He did the surgery once Adam was asleep. God can do surgery on us better when we're resting in His promises and His Word instead of resting in what-ifs and worst-case scenarios.

Write down seven to ten promises that can be ammunition against all the paranoia that comes your way. Then, whenever the fearful, anxious thoughts come to plague you, you have something to combat them with.

REMEMBER—IT'S NOT ABOUT YOU

Have you ever purchased online something you really needed that was *guaranteed* to arrive in two to three business days, only to find yourself still waiting after seventy-two hours? You're left wondering what happened. Why didn't it show up? You look up the tracking information and get an irritating statement saying your package has been stuck in transit.

Let me give you a little perspective. You and I were purchased. We have been blood-bought, purchased by the blood of the Lamb. There is something that God has and desires to use each of us for. There is a work, a mission, a mandate, that He has called us to for His glory.

Here's the thing: It's not about you.

So many of us are disappointed because we have forgotten that life is not about us.

Do you want to be a nicer person? Then recognize that life is not about you! Just think about how much better of a spouse you would be if you really believed that everything you do is for God.

Your job is for His glory. Your money and wealth are for His glory. This opportunity or platform is for His glory. It's not for your ego, for followers, for views, or for likes. Everything you have is truly for His glory.

You and I have been purchased, and this is a blessing that God wants to extend to us. But we can keep this blessing stuck in transit due to our disobedience, laziness, or unbelief. These can all lead to negative thinking.

Is your negative thinking keeping certain opportunities and blessings stuck in transit for you?

Is negative thinking playing a key role in your suffering?

You are not the author. God is.

My last point is to encourage you to render the pen. When you are constantly imagining the worst-case scenarios, you are writing the outcome. But you are not the author! God is! So, give the pen up. Understand that God is the author and the finisher of our faith. Stop trying to control the outcome with your perspective. That's God's job, not yours. So, render the pen.

There are many good ways we can strive to be like Moses, but don't take after him by going back and forth with God about why you don't qualify for His work. When we do that, we're telling God our limitations and making it all about us. Instead, realize that every situation is about His glory and that every outcome is written by His own hand.

QUESTIONS

1. In what areas of your life are you letting fear of failure hold you back? How might God be inviting you to step out of the "shallow end"?
2. How have you been defining success in your life? Does this

definition align with God's Word? What Scripture passages support or challenge your definition?

3. Where in your life are you mislabeling difficulty as impossibility? How might God be using these challenges to strengthen your faith?

4. What "life jacket" of safety is God asking you to take off? What promises from His Word can you hold on to as you step into deeper waters?

PRAYER

Dear Father God, help me stop thinking the worst. Take away any delayed obedience, slothful traits, and negative thinking that have become psychological terrorists against me. Forgive me for being so fearful that I view Your Word and Your principles as electives, God. To be like You is to be fearless. The only fear I want to possess is the reverential fear of You. Help me, God, to be an individual who trusts You versus allowing my mind to listen to the spirit of fear, because You didn't give us that spirit.

Whatever You're asking me to do and whatever instruction You've been putting in my heart, please set me free to pursue it. Help me believe that You have a good plan for me. Please show me what You want me to do. What gift can I offer others or what idea can I birth if there is no worst-case scenario in my mind?

Heavenly Father, please help me recognize that You control outcomes. Help me render the pen so I can stop creating and authoring horrific outcomes, because *You* are the author and finisher of our faith. You're looking for that surrender. Help me to surrender my mind so I can start thinking about what You promised us. God, I ask that You help me to think for Your glory and for Your sake. In Jesus's name, amen.

BONUS CONTENT

To continue rehabbing your heart, use your smartphone to scan the code for a bonus video diving deeper into the content of this chapter.

URL: waterbrookmultnomah.com/HRChapterFive

I'VE GOT CONTROL
ISSUES

"I know the plans I have for you," declares the LORD, "plans to prosper you and not to harm you, plans to give you hope and a future."

—JEREMIAH 29:11

In the last two chapters, we have looked at ways our minds can prevent us from being the people God called us to be. Sometimes our minds are so cluttered that they block God's Word from coming in. We might be able to understand Scripture, but it just isn't registering in a way that shapes our thoughts and actions. Sometimes we fear the worst is going to happen, so we never fulfill the reason we were born. In this chapter, I want to dive a little deeper into why we have anxiety over tomorrow and what that produces.

Do you ever watch the news and begin to worry about what's on the horizon? Do you ever have so much anxiety about what will occur tomorrow that you create impending scenarios in your mind and even physically or emotionally prepare for them to happen? You prepare yourself to get denied. You prepare for that negative doctor's report or for that person to leave. You prepare for people to take advantage of you. You see something unfolding tomorrow that leaves you stuck today.

A LONG MARRIAGE TO CONTROL MAKES SURRENDER FEEL LIKE A DIVORCE

Here is the truth: It's not that you have anxiety over the future or that tomorrow hands you a host of worries. Deep down you really want to control what's going to happen in the future.

That's what causes you to have anxiety. To overthink. To have insomnia and migraines and aches.

The reason you are so stressed is because of your desire to take charge of what happens tomorrow. And this circles back to the last point I made in the previous chapter:

We must learn how to trust the author and finisher of our faith.

Let's be honest. The reason we don't trust God is because we believe our plans are better than His plans. If you look deep down at the motivations and fears you carry about tomorrow, you need to be real about what you're thinking. While you might be reticent to articulate things this way, here is what you are truly thinking when you try to control the future:

I can outline tomorrow's chapter better than God can.

I can narrate the next season or plan what will happen next year better than God can.

When we don't trust the author, we feel as though we have to write the outcomes.

When you've been married to control for so long, surrender to God feels like a divorce.

I know what it's like to want to be in control, so I'm right there with you. I want to determine whether my message is blessing people or not. I want to make sure my wife sees me and my children respond to me in certain ways. I even want to have a say in how many people are reading or listening to this page at this moment! I struggle with control issues just like we all do.

A current struggle impacting my life is how difficult it is for our local church to have services right now. We have five overflows, five shuttles, three golf carts, and four parking lots. When this started happening, I thought, *We can't keep having church like this. The fire marshal said they're going to shut us down.* But we're making it possible. It's hard because we're still growing, but it's not impossible.

There are so many things in our lives that we long to be in charge of: our careers or businesses, our marriages or singleness, our children, our entrepreneurial dreams. Perhaps you want to control how your spouse thinks of you or the quality of your children's faith or the outcome of that dream job you applied for. Here is where this can get us into trouble: Once we realize we *can't* control these things, we often let anxiety and worry control us.

We need to remember Psalm 24:1: "The earth is the LORD's, and everything in it, the world, and all who live in it." The psalmist is reminding us that this earth isn't ours. It belongs to God! Everything we have is just loaned to us. Your house and your car might be paid off, but you are still leasing them from the Lord. Everything you have—your wealth, time, help, strength, marriage, children—everything belongs to your Heavenly Father. You are merely a steward. You own nothing. Even your very breath belongs to the Lord. Control issues come when we forget that we are simply stewards of all God has given us.

My hope is to help you understand how and why you strive to

hold things so tightly. It is often hard to see what God wants for our lives because so many of us have control issues. And when you are married to control, surrender feels like a divorce.

GOD IS A BETTER LORD THAN YOU

One of the most familiar and hope-filled passages of Scripture is Jeremiah 29:11: "'I know the plans I have for you,' declares the LORD, 'plans to prosper you and not to harm you, plans to give you hope and a future.'"

God knows the plan. It's not about you, your efforts, or your strength. Through the prophet Jeremiah, God was telling the people of Israel, *I got this. I already have things organized for your life. I have plans, and they're not bad plans, so you have to trust Me.*

When Jeremiah delivered these words to the Israelites, they were living in exile in Babylon far from their promised home. Jeremiah was pleading with the elders and people of Judah to repent of their sins and turn their hearts back to God. Even though God had revealed that the people's captivity was His judgment for their rebellion and idolatry, He also promised that He had plans for their collective future. In other words, God had beautiful plans for the future of people living under His judgment for their own rebellion. While some false prophets claimed that the Israelites would be quickly released, Jeremiah prophesied that the people would spend many more years in captivity. Yet this passage offers hope and peace by affirming God's larger plan and control even when their immediate circumstances were challenging.

God is in your future *today.* God knows your tomorrow *today.*

Maybe the reason you're so stressed is not because of everything that's going on outside you. Yes, terrible things are happening around us. But perhaps you're stressed because of the warfare that's going on in your heart and mind. Your plan and God's plan are in a battle. That's why you can't sleep or your head hurts, why you're not hungry or you overeat, why you work out so hard but never seem to feel any better, or why you just binge-watch shows. The reason you can never be at peace is because on the inside, your plans and God's plans are at war. You're trying to be God!

Guess what? God is a better Lord than you!

When you want things to turn out a certain way, you're trying to take God's job. Anytime you try to control how things turn out, you are taking on God's work. What you're ultimately telling God is that you don't trust how He will write your story.

For those of us who are waging a war with control issues, Psalm 91:9–16 is a beautiful passage to memorize:

> If you say, "The LORD is my refuge,"
>> and you make the Most High your dwelling,
> no harm will overtake you,
>> no disaster will come near your tent.
> For he will command his angels concerning you
>> to guard you in all your ways;
> they will lift you up in their hands,
>> so that you will not strike your foot against a stone.
> You will tread on the lion and the cobra;
>> you will trample the great lion and the serpent.
> "Because he loves me," says the LORD, "I will rescue him;
>> I will protect him, for he acknowledges my name.
> He will call on me, and I will answer him;
>> I will be with him in trouble,
>> I will deliver him and honor him.
> With long life I will satisfy him
>> and show him my salvation."

In verse 1 of Psalm 91, the psalmist encourages us to "dwell" in the Lord: "Whoever dwells in the shelter of the Most High will rest in the shadow of the Almighty." "Dwells" in Hebrew is *yashab,* which means "to remain" or abide in.[1] So, when you understand that the Lord is your refuge and you make the Most High your root system, no harm will overtake you. God is running things. He is in control. When God is your root system, He nourishes you. God is not just your resource; He is your source.

Deuteronomy 31:8 says, "The LORD, He is the One who goes before you. He will be with you, He will not leave you nor forsake you; do not fear nor be dismayed" (NKJV). This promise helps me remember that I don't need to control anything—because God is in control.

Yet giving up control can be hard. Letting go of that steering wheel or handing over the pen to God can be difficult, especially when things don't go our way.

YOU CAN'T UNLOCK YOUR NEIGHBOR'S DOOR

Sometimes when our ways aren't God's ways, we experience closed doors.

Nobody likes a locked door they can't open.

When God's plan overrides yours, it may come in the form of not getting approved for something or as the end to a relationship. But instead of getting mad about it, maybe step back and realize that God has a plan for this. Maybe God removed someone from your life now so He doesn't have to remove the knife from your back later. He had to disconnect that person because they weren't part of His plan; they were simply a distraction.

It is easy to have distractions in our lives. Sometimes we *allow* people or things to sidetrack us. How do you know whether

---

1. Bible Study Tools, "Yashab," Old Testament Hebrew Lexicon—KJV, biblestudytools.com/lexicons/hebrew/kjv/yashab.html.

someone is a distraction? Their arrival influences your focus on God to depart. They divert you from prayer. Prayer should always be our first response and not our last resort! A distraction causes your purity, your life standards, and your accountability to depart. It's not a lack of focus; it's a mismanagement of your focus. Sure, you're focused, but on the wrong thing!

Giving up our distractions can be hard. When you are out of alignment with God's ways, coming back into alignment can be painful. This especially hurts when it comes in the form of a closed door to something you really want.

But that's *your* plan, not God's.

This is why I so desperately want you to understand that disappointment is for direction, not devastation. That closed door is God simply saying He has a different direction for your life.

We encounter closed doors for a variety of reasons. The most obvious is that God shut a door because it's not His plan—this is not your room to enter. It's like going to your neighbor's house and finding yourself locked out. You can't unlock the door because that's not your house! As Jesus said in John 14:2, "My Father's house has many rooms; if that were not so, would I have told you that I am going there to prepare a place for you?" When a door is shut, our Heavenly Father is telling you that this is not His house, this is not His plan, and this is not your room.

Another reason a door can be shut is that it's not the right time for it to open. You could be trying to give birth to something even though you're just in the first trimester. Or maybe God wants you to become more spiritually mature and grow in biblical intelligence. You may be praying for a blessing, but since God knows that blessings often bring more problems and opposition, He wants you to become stronger in your faith before He opens that door.

Perhaps the door is still shut because you're not hearing Him. You want someone else to tell you what to do, when God is telling you what you already know: *I called you for impact*. He is trying to send you a message: *Stop looking at others and start listening to Me*.

Maybe God knows you're too concerned about what others think versus what He sees. *You still care too much for their applause versus my endorsement*.

You may need to develop further to stop caring what others think. Maybe you need to understand that the only way you can conduct the orchestra is by turning your back on the crowd. God may be calling you to turn your back on something so you can be free and have your identity in Him.

There is a final reason certain doors don't open, and you might not like this one: Some doors stay closed because unlocking them requires your obedience.

Yes, God has grace, and yes, He has mercy. But never confuse His grace with a permission slip to just get by. For some doors you want to go through, obedience is required. Some of us are so frustrated that doors might not be opening for us, but the only cure is repentance from our rebellion.

RECOGNIZE WHAT YOU CAN AND CAN'T CONTROL

The only things you can control are the following:

> Your actions
> Your meditations
> Your words
> Your grind

I say "your meditations" instead of "your thoughts" because the enemy can plant thoughts in our heads. Many kinds of thoughts can flit through our minds. We need wisdom and spiri-

tual discipline to not let them land on the runways of our meditations. You can't always control what thoughts enter your mind,
but you can choose what lands.

And by "your grind," I'm referring to how consistent and intentional you are about something.

Now, the following are things you can't control:

> What people do
> What people think about you
> What people say
> The outcome

WHAT I CAN CONTROL	vs.	WHAT I CAN'T CONTROL
MY ACTIONS		THEIR ACTIONS
MY MEDITATIONS		WHAT THEY THINK ABOUT ME
MY WORDS		WHAT THEY SAY
MY GRIND		THE OUTCOME

If you *could* hold sway over what people did, that would be manipulation or narcissism. You can control neither what someone
does nor what someone thinks about you. It's not your responsibility to try to change their mindset. Some of us are so exhausted
because we're trying to re-create other people's mental versions of
us! Forget trying to do that—you have no control over that.

CONTROL ISSUES ARE OUR ATTEMPTS
TO HAVE SOVEREIGNTY

I have noticed something about those of us who desire to be in
control:

We are easily angered.

Often, a short fuse indicates that you want to be in command. Anger and control are siblings. You get so angry because this is not the way you want things to go, people aren't cooperating, or you can't determine the results.

Controlling people are usually patience deprived. I define patience as the ability to accept that things are going differently than what we had in mind. When heavy traffic is making you late yet you can't accept that this looks different from your plans, that means you lack patience. Or when you're looking over someone's shoulder and micromanaging them, whether it's an employee, a spouse, or a child, you're low on patience—you are trying to control things.

You have the power to choose how you respond when things don't go your way. Reining in your response does not mean you're avoiding your emotions; rather, you are choosing to not let your emotions dictate your response.

There is a fine line between perfectionism and narcissism. The line is so thin, in fact, that sometimes we cross it and don't even know it. If you want things to be perfect and go exactly one way, you will exhaust yourself trying to control everything, including anyone you interreact with. Anybody who battles with perfectionism will find themselves snapping at people who don't do things the way they want them done. This motivation and desire for control can easily lead to narcissism, where you no longer lack empathy and instead carry a sense of entitlement.

This is why your healing matters so deeply. When you're wounded, you'll label narcissism as love and then begin to make excuses, or you'll mislabel how someone acts, because deep down, you want to control things. You want to fill the void or avoid the mistake or fix the problem. But the only One who can do all those things is God. Surrender everything to Him, including all the things you *think* you can control but can't.

REASONS

Why do we want to control things so badly? There are two primary reasons: fear and woundedness from past experiences.

Fear is the main driver behind our need to be in control. Fear first shows up in seed form. Our meditations and our mental scenarios then transition it from seed into a mature crop. This fear can manifest in various ways—like micromanaging our children because we're afraid of what might happen, or overworking because we fear being stuck in the financial insecurity from our childhood.

Fear causes us to forget that everything belongs to the Lord, including our children and our work. It makes us forget our dreams and forgo taking risks.

Maybe God put us in the boat so we would take a risk and step out of it. Yet fear causes us to swing back to shore without ever experiencing walking in the deep.

Are you afraid of what will happen because the unknown terrifies you?

Fear is not trusting that God will protect you better than you could protect yourself.

The second reason we long for control is our experience of childhood trauma. This is the story of many people I've met. So many of us struggle to let go and trust God because our parents were wounded souls. When you grow up unable to trust your caregivers, you often carry that distrust into adulthood. This results in having trust and control issues.

Maybe you were abused, so it's hard for you to trust others.

Perhaps your single mother had several jobs, so you were responsible to take care of your younger siblings. So instead of learning what it feels like to be loved, you learned what it feels like to be needed.

Brothers, maybe you never received affirmations or affection from your parents, so now you easily feel rejected by the people around you. If that feels familiar, you might be looking for the love you didn't get from your parents in places you shouldn't be looking.

Sisters, maybe your daddy broke your heart before any man ever did, so now you're trying to control your husband.

This is why it is essential to deal with unresolved childhood pain.

We may try to control our healing, but ultimately God is the only One who can heal us.

HIRE AND FIRE ACCORDINGLY

We've all been heartbroken. But when heartbreak goes unaddressed and untreated, it leads to paranoia. Here's why: Heartbreak affects your perspective. It affects how you respond to people and problems. It also affects your sleep and your decision-making.

If you aren't intentional with your healing, heartbreak will hand you paranoia:

I can't do this.
What's going to happen now?
I don't trust this.

Then what?

After you swim in the water of dysfunction for a while, peace will feel like a trigger. Paranoia can sit on your heart for so long that discovering any healing can seem impossible. When paranoia is giving you directions, it's hard to discover the lanes that lead to healing. You must shift your perspective and decide that paranoia will not rule your heart.

Not today, paranoia. Today growth is gonna start happening!
Today those chains are gonna start breaking!
Today my perspective is gonna begin to shift!

This is not something that happens overnight. The only thing that seems to pop up overnight is a mushroom. We're not trying to grow fungus.

What we want to have is *Godfidence.* Not just confidence in our own abilities, gifts, and pursuits—confidence in God. I want you to have confidence in God's ability, gifts, and pursuits as you seek to grow and heal.

Godfidence.

God made you to be the district manager over the department of your peace, so you have to hire and fire accordingly. You need to hire people, coaches, places, and things that are conducive to your healing. And you need to let go of those people who are committed to misunderstanding you, whom you have to always overexplain yourself to. But it will be hard for you to hire and fire accordingly if paranoia sits on the throne of your heart.

Don't let paranoia direct those decisions. Understand that you can't change people; that is God's job. Your husband or wife changing—that's God's job. Let God work on the people in your life while you focus on you.

MANY WANT TO BE DISCOVERED; FEW WANT TO BE DEVELOPED

"Your blessing is on the way!"

How many times have you heard a pastor proclaim this?

I believe we have done people a disservice. We have over-preached messages about how it is *your* season. "You have finally arrived!" "Now is your time!" We have preached that so much that we've conditioned people not to value the offseasons.

We live in an era of influencers and moguls. Our culture has a chronic obsession with followers, subscriptions, likes, and views. We no longer value development. Many people want to be discovered; few people want to be developed. So many of our prayers orbit around the theme of being discovered or discovering something, but they rarely center on being developed.

Maybe it's just me, but I believe it is better for me to be overdeveloped and underexposed than overexposed and underdeveloped.

What if we valued development? What if we valued the offseason?

The offseason is when nobody knows your name but you're in training. It can feel like the season of obscurity.

The offseason is where you practice. It's where you develop your professional gifts.

It's too late to learn how to use your slingshot when Goliath is standing right across the field. It is too late for you to conjure up and develop a prayer life when you're about to be thrown into the lions' den.

The offseason is what I like to call therapeutic sanctification. *Therapeutic* relates to treating or providing healing, while *sanctification* is the act of setting apart for special use. God wants you to heal and get the treatment you need. Why? Because He has a special use and assignment for you. If it weren't special, you wouldn't have a birthday. The fact that you have a birthday—and that you are still here and have a pulse—means there is a particular work that God has given only you to do. Embrace the offseason so you can get the healing and the practice you need.

GOD DEALS WITH OUR JACOBS AT NIGHT, NOT AT NOON

In the Bible, name changes often symbolize a significant transformation or new phase in a person's life, especially in their relationship with God. Here are three examples from Genesis:

Abraham: In Genesis 17:5, God changed Abram's name to Abraham, meaning "father of a multitude."[2] This new name reflected God's covenant with Abraham, promising that he would be the father of a great number of people and the ancestor of many nations.

Sarah: Sarai's name became Sarah, meaning "princess" or "noblewoman,"[3] reflecting her new role as the mother of nations and kings. This name change also signified God's promise that she would bear a child, Isaac, despite her old age (17:15, 19).

Israel: After Jacob wrestled with an angel, God changed his name to Israel, meaning "he who struggles with God" or "God prevails."[4] This marked a turning point in Jacob's life, symbolizing his spiritual transformation and the establishment of his descendants, the Israelites, as God's chosen people (32:28).

Each of these name changes signified a divine purpose and a new identity in God's plan for the person.

2. Blue Letter Bible, "Abraham," blueletterbible.org/lexicon/h85/esv/wlc/0-1/.

3. Blue Letter Bible, "Sarah," blueletterbible.org/lexicon/h8283/esv/wlc/0-1/.

4. "The Symbolism of Israel: Biblical Perspectives and Historical Significance," Digital Bible, November 24, 2023, digitalbible.ca/article-page/bible-study-symbols-the-symbolism-of-israel-biblical-perspectives-and-historical-significance-1700845108130x282793340323530980.

So, let me use some theological verbiage on you: God wants to deal with your Jacob.

Ever heard that expression?

God has to place many of us in offseasons to deal with the Jacob that resides in each person. Let's look at the passage of Scripture where Jacob wrestles with God, starting in Genesis 32:22–23:

> He arose that night and took his two wives, his two female servants, and his eleven sons, and crossed over the ford of Jabbok. He took them, sent them over the brook, and sent over what he had. (NKJV)

It's essential to see what Jacob is doing here. He is putting in front of him all his valuable possessions, all the things that are important to him. I highlight this because it's what a lot of us do. We put forth our gifts to hide our inner Jacobs. Yes, people can see your giftedness, but nobody can see the inner struggles you're battling. Nobody knows what you are really dealing with in the dark. Except God. And God wants to deal with that inner Jacob:

> Then Jacob was left alone; and a Man wrestled with him until the breaking of day. Now when He saw that He did not prevail against him, He touched the socket of his hip; and the socket of Jacob's hip was out of joint as He wrestled with him. And He said, "Let Me go, for the day breaks."
>
> But he said, "I will not let You go unless You bless me!" (verses 24–26, NKJV)

This is powerful because so many of us are in a dark place wrestling with something, yet nobody knows about it. People see our pretty posts on the socials and observe our talents and abilities, but nobody sees us wrestling in the dark. Jacob's wrestling in the dark is symbolic of what's going on inside him. But when daybreak comes, it literally dawns on Jacob whom he is fighting:

I'm wrestling with God.

Can you see the comparison to what we do so often?

I'm wrestling to try to heal from this, to forgive them.

I'm wrestling with my anger, with my bitterness.

But really, whom are you wrestling with? Whom are you trying to control and contain with your own hands?

We are wrestling with the One who can heal us from all these things.

When Jacob realizes this, he switches from wrestling to holding. "I will not let You go unless You bless me," he says.

The blessing comes in the holding, not the wrestling:

> So He said to him, "What is your name?"
>
> He said, "Jacob."
>
> And He said, "Your name shall no longer be called Jacob, but Israel; for you have struggled with God and with men, and have prevailed." (verses 27–28, NKJV)

The question "What is your name?" essentially means "What is your struggle?" What are you dealing with in the dark? What have you hidden behind your gift? What have you been hiding behind your posts? God wants to deal with the person behind the keyboard, not just the person in the frame. He wants to be with you.

The name Jacob means "he grasps the heel," which is a Hebrew idiom for "he deceives" (35:10, footnote). So, in this confrontation with God, Jacob is finally coming to grips with what he's been battling his whole life. He was the one who stole his older brother Esau's birthright by lying to his father. And the theme of deception has remained in Jacob's life. This is the night Jacob finally wrestles with this.

A lot of us have become masters at hiding behind what we present to the rest of the world. In the dark, we're wrestling. There is a Jacob inside me and a Jacob inside you. I can't speak for anybody else, but I'm grateful that God deals with our Jacobs at night and not at noon! Nobody knows about it except God.

Yes, people are going to judge you by your Jacob, but God knows you have an Israel inside you. That's why He sends you into the offseason. You need a name change.

So, what is your struggle? What are you wrestling with in the dark?

Are you wrestling with God and refusing to let Him heal you?

Are you worried about tomorrow while refusing to wait for the Lord?

Are you willing to simply let go and cling to Him?

KNOW WHAT GOD CONTROLS AND WHAT WE CONTROL

The following chart shows what God controls versus what we control.

WHAT GOD CONTROLS vs.	WHAT I CONTROL
THE OUTCOME	MY OBEDIENCE
THE DOOR	MY EFFORTS
THE CHANGE	MY POSTURE
THE WIDTH	MY EXCELLENCE

God controls outcomes. You control your obedience.

No matter how hard you push or how hard you grind, God presides over every open and closed door. The only thing you can command is your effort.

God controls transformations. You can't change people or situations. You can't even make the season change. The only thing you can alter is your posture.

God governs the width of a thing, meaning how far it reaches. How influential or impactful something is or how many followers you get—all of that is God's doing. Our focus is simply to do our best.

STOP TRYING TO CARRY GOD-WEIGHT

Here are a few basic tips to help us war against our control issues.

First, we must trust that God will never let us drown. No matter how dire or frightening a situation might appear, He will always be our refuge. Believe that. When the Lord is our shelter and our root system is in Him, He will uphold us. Our faith might falter, just as Peter's did when he tried to walk on water, but even then, God is there to catch us. Believing this truth can anchor us in moments of uncertainty.

Second, to battle control issues, we must unlearn a shortage mentality. Stop thinking that if an opportunity fell through, you missed out. Heaven doesn't have a shortage! Remember, God knows the plan He has for you (Jeremiah 29:11). There is no deficiency in His plan. What God wants you to have will never be on back order. It is on reserve until you get there—until the offseason shifts to the regular season and until your obedience.

Third, cast your cares on God. Whatever is bothering you, cast it on Him.

We bought a television so our children could watch cartoons on it. To set up the parental controls over what they watched, I needed to use a number on the screen to cast my phone to the TV. I tried to do this, but for some reason my phone wasn't connecting. I couldn't figure out why until I pushed the information button—and learned that my phone had to be on the same internet network as the television.

A lot of us aren't on the same network that God has for our lives. We are not aligned with His plan. So, the reason you can't cast your cares on Him is that you don't trust Him. You're casting your cares on your boyfriend or your girlfriend, your friends or your colleagues—everybody else but Him.

We need to cast our cares on God, and the only way we can do that is to be on the same network with Him. Our spirits have to be aligned with what He desires for us so we won't be frustrated and have no connection with Him.

Finally, to overcome our control issues, we have to trust that God is good at His job—that He is good at being God. He is a good, good God. Stop trying to carry around God-weight. That's His responsibility, not yours. Don't attempt to be in the driver's seat. Surrender the wheel. Just let go.

Those roads that scare you or look fearful? Trust Him.

The roads that are a little bumpy? Trust Him.

The routes you didn't know you would travel down? Trust Him.

Trust God more than you trust yourself, and surrender the wheel to Him.

QUESTIONS

1. What areas of your life do you find most difficult to surrender to God? Why do you think these particular areas are challenging for you?

2. How has your desire for control affected your relationships with others? With God?

3. What closed doors in your life might actually be God's protection rather than His rejection? How might your perspective change if you viewed them this way?

4. What practical steps can you take this week to surrender control in one area of your life? How can you remind yourself that "God is a better Lord than you"?

PRAYER

Dear Heavenly Father, help me remember that You control the outcome. I trust You more than my own efforts. Right now, I surrender everything to You. I want to be in the driver's seat and to be the author of my story, but that's Your job, and You're better at it. Help me, God, to stop hiding behind my gifts and to see what I'm really dealing with in the dark. Help me to start holding on to You and every promise You've given me. Help me fall in love with You and hold on to Your promises more than I want to be in control. I let go of the wheel. In Jesus's name, amen.

BONUS CONTENT

To continue rehabbing your heart, use your smartphone to scan the code for a bonus video diving deeper into the content of this chapter.

URL: waterbrookmultnomah.com/HRChapterSix

SEVEN

IT'S NOT PERSONAL; IT'S SPIRITUAL

Paul, greatly annoyed, turned and said to the spirit, "I command you in the name of Jesus Christ to come out of her." And he came out that very hour. But when her masters saw that their hope of profit was gone, they seized Paul and Silas and dragged them into the marketplace to the authorities.

—ACTS 16:18–19 (NKJV)

In the spring of 2023, my wife's doctor asked the same question she had asked me two other times. My beautiful bride and I were expecting our third baby that April, and we couldn't wait to meet our second son, Josiah Zion Flowers.

"Okay, Daddy," the doctor said. "Do you want to cut the umbilical cord?"

Now, when our daughter, Melody, was born, as excited as I was to become a father for the first time, I had said, "No, thank you." I also said no when the doctor asked this for our son Jerry III. I didn't want any birth defects to be my doing! But this time, I decided I wanted to do it. I wanted to remind myself that the father has the authority to cut.

GOD ORDERS NOT ONLY OUR STEPS
BUT ALSO OUR STOPS

At times, there is stuff our Heavenly Father wants to prune out of our lives. He cuts us so He can keep us.

The obvious reason I cut the umbilical cord for my son was so that I could keep him and take him home with us. That cord needed to be severed so I could have the joy and experience of burping our son and raising him and teaching him kingdom principles.

When God wants to do something with you, He might require something to be snipped from your life to do it.

I want to take you deeper, God might be telling you. But something has to be cut.

I want to take you higher. I want to increase your anointing.

But something has to be cut. And the Father has the authority to do that.

Is it time for God to cut something from you? What risk do you need to take in your life to see His wonders? Have you had enough with swimming in the shallow end of casual Christianity?

God didn't build you for ponds. He built you for oceans!

You can never experience the miracle of walking on water if you stay on the shore of your logic. But that might mean God lets you be cut. He doesn't want to hurt us; rather, He lets us experience cuts to keep us in His presence and in His will.

I had to cut the umbilical cord to keep my son. This represents what Jesus said in John 15:2: "He cuts off every branch in me that bears no fruit, while every branch that does bear fruit he prunes so that it will be even more fruitful."

Remember, "the steps of a good man are ordered by the LORD" (Psalm 37:23, NKJV). But let me throw this out there: God does not just order our steps. He also orders our stops.

Here's a thought that might mess you up. Some of you are hurting from losing stuff that was never yours—things that were never God's will or part of His plan.

God doesn't cut you to hurt you. He does it to keep you.

You see, it's not personal; it's spiritual. This is what I want us to discover in this chapter. How can you be birthed into a whole nother dimension of discernment? How can you know whether something in your life must be cut? Yes, this might hurt your heart, but God is going to do it to grow you and your spirit.

Let's return to a theme I covered in chapter 4 about all the voices inside your head.

LEASING YOUR EAR TO SOMEONE IS LICENSING THEM TO OPERATE ON YOU

Do you ever feel like there's a war in your soul?

Do you ever feel like your life verse is Romans 7:19? "I do not do the good I want to do, but the evil I do not want to do—this I keep on doing." Do you wake up quoting verse 24: "What a wretched man I am! Who will rescue me from this body that is subject to death?"

We can spend every day wrestling with ourselves because we each carry a weapon of mass destruction (WMD) around. This is not a bomb or a grenade. It's not an AR-15 or a 9mm handgun.

This undetected weapon that hell is using is a microphone.

Every day, this spiritual WMD amplifies the voices of spiritual garbage. It stifles our spiritual growth and suffocates our spiritual development. This mic blasts the voices of the spiritually ignorant and makes them popular. These masses justify the favorite things in our lives: certain playlists, podcasts, shows to stream, songs.

The thing is, we love to watch shows saturated with the sins that Jesus died for. We love to listen to songs that display the very reason He hung and bled on the cross.

The weapon of spiritual mass destruction is often a mic.

The voices of spiritual heresy share popular messages that we love to hear. "It's your season," they claim. "Your blessing is on the way!" This mic doesn't share messages that plead for us to turn to Jesus, nor does it give us sound, biblical doctrine. It doesn't amplify messages that cause us to recognize that we must surrender our own wills to the will of Yahweh. We don't hear messages that urge us toward repentance, that lead us to chop down the trees of our rebellion and beg for God to uproot our sin.

The enemy we wrestle with is slick. The old serpent is sly. He says, "Okay, if I can't stop you, then I'll stall you. And while you're stalled, I will amplify the voices that will have you binging on things you shouldn't be listening to." That is Satan's strategy. He wants to add many voices to the microphone in your soul—the part of yourself that involves the mind, will, emotions, imagination, and reasoning.

The enemy wants to place multiple voices on the mic of your soul so that the voice of your Good Shepherd has to compete with all the others.

God is talking to you, but perhaps so are depression, anxiety, and trauma.

So are lust and pride.

We end up with so many voices talking that we can't hear our Good Shepherd. He has to compete with all those other voices the enemy has amplified. Satan does this to birth confusion inside us so that questions continually rage in our minds:

Is that God, or is that me? Is it Him or narcissism?
Is that God, or is it the spirit of fear?
Is that God, or is that what my ex said? What my ex-pastor said?
Is that God, or is it just what I've been taught to believe?

All those amplified voices play on massive sound systems inside the concert halls of our minds, keeping us from ever hearing God speak to us.

I view this as a demonic math equation. This chart shows how it works:

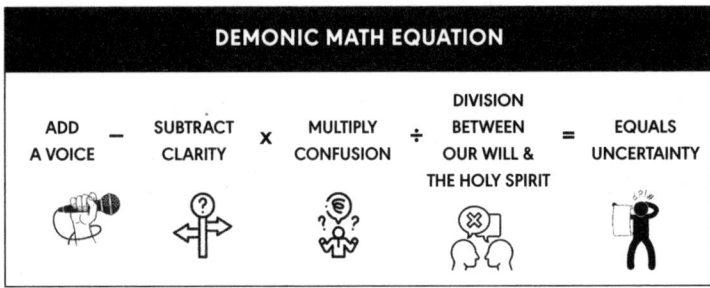

The devil wants to *add a voice* so he can *subtract clarity.* This will *multiply confusion* and then cause *division between our will and the Holy Spirit,* which *equals uncertainty.*

Every voice that is amplified in your mind only diminishes your clarity. This multiplies the confusion and chaos inside you, causing your will to separate from the will of the Holy Spirit. All of this becomes the uncertainty that can suffocate us.

So, why does the devil do this? I believe it's for two reasons. First, the enemy wants us to listen to the wrong voices all the time. He knows this truth: Whatever or whomever you lease your ear to consistently is what or whom you are licensing to operate on you. In other words, they are a deposit of how your next season will look.

Let's look at some of these voices, starting in Jeremiah 23:16.

This is what the LORD Almighty says:
"Do not listen to what the prophets are prophesying to you;
    they fill you with false hopes.
They speak visions from their own minds,
    not from the mouth of the LORD."

Bad doctrine is a perversion of hope; it moves people to hope in God to do what the Bible never says He would do:

> They keep saying to those who despise me,
>> "The LORD says: You will have peace."
> And to all who follow the stubbornness of their hearts
>> they say, "No harm will come to you." (verse 17)

Doesn't this sound like 85 percent of the preaching in America on Sunday? "It's your season!" "It's your time!" "Your breakthrough is on the way!" "Your harvest is coming!" But we don't address the stubbornness of our hearts. We don't talk about sin from pulpits anymore. And we most certainly don't talk about hell.

Pastors want to preach about peace, not about how hell is a real place of God's wrath that was never made for us but for Satan and his demons. We want to hear sermons about no harm ever finding us—not about how if we reject the gospel and God, He abides by our decisions. Here's the reality: The reason people go to hell is not because God doesn't love them. The truth is that God loves us so much that He respects our will. He would be an unloving God if He forced people to live with Him for all eternity who choose not to seek His face or pray to Him. Hell is God saying, *I respect your choice to not want Me.*

Why don't we preach this stuff anymore? Why don't we quote one of the most haunting passages of Scripture, where God says, "I never knew you; depart from Me, you who practice lawlessness!" (Matthew 7:23, NKJV)? Why don't we describe an eternity in a place full of burning sulfur, a prison of suffocating gas, as in Revelation 20:10: "The devil, who deceived them, was thrown into the lake of burning sulfur, where the beast and the false prophet had been thrown. They will be tormented day and night for ever and ever"? Why don't we refer to the place Matthew 10:28 talks about: "Do not fear those who kill the body but cannot kill the soul. But rather fear Him who is able to destroy both soul and body in hell" (NKJV)?

Let's continue in Jeremiah 23:18–20, where God speaks a word of judgment on the false prophets misleading the people of Israel:

> Which of them has stood in the council of the LORD
>> to see or to hear his word?
>> Who has listened and heard his word?
> See, the storm of the LORD
>> will burst out in wrath,
> a whirlwind swirling down
>> on the heads of the wicked.
> The anger of the LORD will not turn back
>> until he fully accomplishes
>> the purposes of his heart.
> In days to come
>> you will understand it clearly.

We need to make sure that the voices we are listening to—even those from the pulpit—are speaking truth. We can sense it in our spirits. There are preachers who are taking advantage of people for their own gain, using people's trauma for their monetization.

Again, whatever or whomever you lease your ear to consistently—that you are listening to on a regular basis—is the thing or person you are licensing to operate on you. The enemy wants to add voices to your life to multiply your confusion.

The second reason Satan has this demonic math equation, adding multiple voices to the mics inside us, is to get us to mislabel those voices we hear. Then we end up confused and uncertain.

We might label the voice of fear as a voice of wisdom. "I don't think it's financially wise for us to break up." "I don't think it's wise to start working on that book." "The smartest thing for me to do is to stay in this job." The spirit of fear keeps us stuck because we label it as the voice of wisdom.

We can label trauma as our personality. "That's just who I am." But no, this is who you are *now*. This is who you *became* due to who they were! This is the residue of that divorce or breakup, the residue of childhood trauma, church hurt, or abandonment. Now, I want to warn you—I am about to mention some very sensitive issues that have deeply impacted people in my church: rape and molestation. I want you to know that the residue of that molestation, of that rape, does not define you. If you've experienced this level of trauma, I encourage you to seek out the guidance of a professional counselor. However, I also want you to know that your heart absolutely can be healed.

This is not who you are. But the enemy tells you otherwise. He adds multiple voices to the microphone in your soul so that you mislabel them.

"God told me my season is up." No, actually you just got offended by the sermon you heard, and now you want to leave the church.

"God is telling me I should go into business with these people." No, all you are longing for is more money.

"God is calling me to this ministry." No, you just want a bigger platform and a larger following.

The Good Shepherd tries to talk with us every day, but His voice competes with all these other amplified voices. Doubt, pride, fear, trauma—all these voices are vying for your attention. They are shouting inside your head.

What are you called to do? It's simple.

You need to release those voices!

WHEN YOU DON'T PROTECT YOUR SPIRIT, YOU INVITE SPIRITUAL GRAFFITI

Satan wants you to stay stuck in the sound room of your dissenting voices, keeping you confused and isolated and immature in your walk with Christ. But once you start moving and begin to intentionally seek growth, spiritual warfare will be activated. The story of Paul and Silas in Acts 16:16–19 is a good example of this:

> Now it happened, as we went to prayer, that a certain slave girl possessed with a spirit of divination met us, who brought her masters much profit by fortune-telling. This girl followed Paul and us, and cried out, saying, "These men are the servants of the Most High God, who proclaim to us the way of salvation." And this she did for many days.
>
> But Paul, greatly annoyed, turned and said to the spirit, "I command you in the name of Jesus Christ to come out of her." And he came out that very hour. But when her masters saw that their hope of profit was gone, they seized Paul and Silas and dragged them into the marketplace to the authorities. (NKJV)

The original Greek word for "spirit of divination" is *python,*[1] meaning this spirit was like a python snake. Let's look at two types of serpents: the viper and the python. When vipers strike, they put venom in your blood. Spiritually, the devil can inject something into your bloodline. There can be a generational cycle or a negative trait your mother or grandaddy had that the enemy thinks will work on you. This is how vipers kill. Pythons, how-

1. Blue Letter Bible, *"python,"* blueletterbible.org/lexicon/g4436/esv/mgnt/0-1/.

ever, kill by attaching and squeezing. A python spirit kills by putting a stranglehold on you.

As Paul and Silas were walking, this girl kept hollering behind them: "Listen to them! Listen to these servants of God!" This demonstrates why you must be careful about who supports you. Some are bound by people-pleasing or by selfish needs or ambition. The young woman was calling others to listen to Paul and Silas, but this was the support of the devil. So, why was this spirit of divination or spirit of python following and harassing them? Because that's what pythons do—they attach and twist around us. This is what Satan tries to do to us.

The enemy tries to attach himself to your dreams and thought patterns and preferences. That's the way he's looking to strike and kill you.

Verse 18 in the NKJV says Paul was "greatly annoyed." Other translations say "grieved" or "exasperated" or "aggravated."[2] This sort of annoyance and grief and exasperation can happen to us as well. Some of us get annoyed not because of our next-door neighbors or the tacos we ate last night or because we didn't get enough sleep. It's because our spirits are grieving, and this grieving manifests in our bodies. Your spirit is asking, "How long are you going to continue to allow these voices access to you?"

Do you ever find yourself annoyed with a python spirit residing inside you? Maybe it's your routine of laziness or a divorce in your family. Maybe you're annoyed because you keep picking the same wrong person only with a different name. Perhaps you're annoyed with an addiction or a substance dependence that triumphs over having a devotion dependence.

If you're annoyed like Paul was, then follow his example of turning around and saying to the spirit, "I command you in the name of Jesus Christ to come out."

2. Bible Hub, "Acts 16:18," biblehub.com/acts/16-18.htm.

If you are battling depression or wrestling with anxiety, you can be released in the name of Jesus.

If you don't have clarity because it feels like your vision is fogged, you can be released in the name of Jesus.

Remember: It's not personal; it's spiritual. Maybe you need to activate your spiritual awareness.

The reason a lot of us spend our lives so annoyed, grieved, and frustrated that we're not receiving the results we desire is because we try to achieve the right thing from the wrong place or the wrong level. We try to fight these things with willpower, but willpower doesn't work. We need His power! We must learn how to both fight and worship from our spirits. The Father is seeking those who know how to worship Him "in spirit and truth" (John 4:24, NKJV).

Sin always reveals an area where a need is deprived. If we really evaluated what is tempting us, we would see areas of famine in our lives. *I don't get the affirmations I need. So, I'm quick to fall to a counterfeit because when someone seems to affirm me, they're feeding and watering something that's already in drought inside me.* Sin exposes areas that are in need. Unfortunately, we usually seek out the sinful, temporary, fleeting pleasure versus the spiritual, soul-quenching fulfillment that can be found only in Jesus.

Do you ever cry out from your spirit?

Do you protect your spirit?

If you cannot recognize when something is spiritual and if you don't know how to protect your spirit, you invite spiritual graffiti. Anybody can mark and paint on you. In other words, anybody can distract you. Anybody can bleed on you.

For some, the annoyance you feel inside is your spirit asking, "How long? How long will you continue to ignore my instruction? How long will you allow that counterfeit to have access to you? How long will you let the enemy talk you out of what God is trying to talk you into? How long will you allow a lie to keep you comfortable?"

So many of us have settled for polluted wells when God is calling us to fresh springs.

The moment you decide to no longer be annoyed and to let Jesus release you, there will be a change that a lot of people might not like. You will have to reach a place of unavailability with certain people and places, communicating, "I'm unavailable to your toxicity. I'm unavailable to your drama. I'm not trying to be mean. It's not personal; it's spiritual."

Getting this spiritual insight will cause some to misjudge you. When you decide to protect your spirit and change who you are, certain people will struggle because of who you've been.

Become annoyed enough to be unavailable.

Have the courage to be disliked.

Have the boldness to not be bound by what others think about you.

When we realize it's not personal but spiritual, that spiritual awareness will cause our lives to expand. We will leave our casual Christianity behind.

The enemy wants to prevent that. So, he's going to do everything he can to pull that spirit back down.

YOUR SPIRIT IS THE ETHERNET CORD TO GOD

What does the enemy really want? How does he attack us?

The enemy's goal is to make you heavy in spirit. Satan wants you to have to carry around a spirit of heaviness. One word for "burden" in the Greek is *baros,* which means a weight or a heavy burden.[3] That is the spirit of heaviness. Something is overwhelming you on the inside.

When the enemy attacks you in the spirit, it will often mani-

3. Bible Hub, "922. *baros,*" biblehub.com/greek/922.htm.

fest in your mind and heart, which then expands to your body. This results in things like weight gain or loss, hair loss, wrinkles— whatever it may be. But Satan's goal is to try to crush your spirit. He wants you to get stuck by what happened in your past.

Ephesians 6:12 explains whom we ultimately contend with every day: "We wrestle not against flesh and blood, but against principalities, against powers, against the rulers of the darkness of this world, against spiritual wickedness in high places" (KJV). This is the battle taking place in the realm we can't see with the natural eye.

You might have been wounded by a parent, a pastor, or an ex, but they were just puppets. You're not wrestling with those people. Remember, it's not personal; it's spiritual. The enemy may have used those people to attack your spirit. He wages a war against your spirit, which then manifests in the mind and the heart. Your mind begins to think unhealthy thoughts, your heart fears feeling betrayed or let down again, and this manifests itself in your body.

We are all aware of our bodies. When it's cold out, we put on sweatshirts. When something is loud, we cover our ears. This is the body. The soul is the part of you that houses your mind, will, emotions, and imagination. Your spirit is your connection to God. In fact, I describe the human spirit as an Ethernet cord to God. It's how you download revelation from God and upload worship to Him. Without God, you can have a body and a soul, but spiritually you're dead.

Throughout the Scriptures, the words *soul* and *spirit* are not always interchangeable. An example of this is in Hebrews 4:12:

> The word of God is living and powerful, and sharper than any two-edged sword, piercing even to the division of soul and spirit, and of joints and marrow,

and is a discerner of the thoughts and intents of the heart. (NKJV)

The writer of Hebrews is saying that certain things in Scripture will not sit well with our souls but will edify our spirits. The Word of God pierces "even to the division of soul and spirit." This means your soul wants to continue doing some things, but your spirit knows they are not good for you and says, "Not anymore!"

Even though there are certain things your mind and emotions may like, your spirit might be telling you that they're unhealthy. That's why the enemy attacks our spirits. He wants to break our Ethernet cords to God so we can't download anything from Him to upload into our souls and manifest out of our bodies. Satan couldn't care less about your job or your car. He wants to affect your spirit because that is where your faith resides, your worship exists, and your wholeness is held. That is where the real *you* lives. Yes, we are humans, but we are also spirit beings. When we die, our spirits will go back to God. So, our bodies are just tents. That's all they are. Ultimately, then, the enemy wants to get inside your tent and crush your spirit.

HELL IS TERRIFIED WHEN YOU REJOICE AMID CHAOS

So, how do you fend off the enemy when he comes after your spirit? How do you combat all those voices inside you? How do you stand up to the python spirit and let Jesus release you from its grip? I want to show you how to fight back, because you never know when a simple choice you make will be a destiny moment that impacts a lot of things.

Our lives are filled with so many voices and so many choices every single day. Yet at times, you and I are going to stand in front of a destiny moment—one of those times when whatever choice you make and whatever voice you listen to will have an impact on your destiny. This isn't the sort of choice you can take lightly, the kind you simply flip a coin and pick heads or tails for. This choice is going to affect your peace and your joy meter. It will impact your bloodline. We must be people who can discern demonic distractions from destiny moments.

You can't take destiny steps while simultaneously listening to the wrong voice.

You can't be who you're called to be and who you used to be at the same time.

You can't hold on to your upward calling and still flirt with your downward craving.

The enemy—the spirit of the python—slides and twists around us to make us think that we can want both him and God. We believe that we can represent Jesus in public but play with the enemy in private. That python will attach himself to us and twist our thoughts, so we need to know how to fight back.

First Thessalonians 5:16–18 provides us with the instruction we need: "Rejoice always, pray continually, give thanks in all circumstances; for this is God's will for you in Christ Jesus."

I've read and heard this scripture so many times, but it takes on a whole new meaning to me in the context of this chapter—especially when we think about the mic we are always listening to in our minds. The instructions here are simple and straightforward, starting with this first command:

Rejoice always.

How many of us read Bible passages but selectively walk them out? I wonder what my generation would look like if we viewed Scripture as principles and commands versus electives and suggestions.

So, why does Paul command us to rejoice in the Lord? It's because the opposite of rejoicing is regret, and *regret* means to mourn. Mourning tunes in to the frequency of sadness, and after sadness speaks into the mic in our minds for an extended time, it makes space for despair. Once despair is at the mic for a while, it makes space for hopelessness. And hopelessness makes space for the voice of suicide.

What happens when we rejoice instead? Rejoicing removes a voice! This is how we engage in spiritual warfare. Joy and sorrow can't share the microphone. So, if we can learn to rejoice always, that joy will veto any negative voices alongside it.

Some of you are going through fiery trials where joy seems like the last thing you can feel. Here is another instruction for you from 1 Peter 4:12–13:

> Beloved, do not think it strange concerning the fiery trial which is to try you, as though some strange thing happened to you; but rejoice to the extent that you partake of Christ's sufferings, that when His glory is revealed, you may also be glad with exceeding joy. (NKJV)

Maybe you're going through one of those trials right now. You are hearing a whole host of voices at the mic: despair and doubt and sadness and hopelessness. If so, let me encourage you to remove those voices by rejoicing! Be full of joy as you tell those other voices to go away.

Pride, you gotta go.
Arrogance, get out of here.
Sorrow and oppression and insomnia, you know where to go.
Depression and trauma, I'm gonna take whatever steps necessary to get you evicted from my soul! If that's therapy or counseling or grief sessions, it doesn't matter. You're getting evicted!

Rejoicing disconnects all these voices.

Hell gets terrified when you rejoice in the midst of chaos. The enemy becomes alarmed when you are full of joy even though your situation looks bad.

I'm not praising God because of what I'm facing; I'm praising God because He is that good. Because He is holy and wonderful and righteous.

I'm praising God because I know God's got me.

Don't you dare allow your situation to mute God's voice! Rejoicing removes the enemy's voices.

DON'T LET THE ENEMY HIDE IN PLAIN SIGHT

It's not personal; it's spiritual. So, how do we become spiritually healthy?

Spiritual health doesn't happen by accident. It requires exposure and cultivation. We need to *see* the things that are spiritually healthy for us and then nurture and develop them. The first part is easy. It's the second part that's more difficult.

How do you cultivate spiritual health? You have hard and uncomfortable conversations. You are willing to unlearn unhealthy habits. You become intentional with your spiritual growth and your spiritual healing.

You also use the power of recognition.

When thieves target a house, they usually wear masks. That's because if you can recognize them, you can trace them. If you know what the thieves look like, then you can spot them and identify who they are.

In the same way, if you can recognize an unhealthy habit or trait, then you can trace it to its beginning. Deliverance is not just stopping the act. It's discovering how it started.

Do you have some thieves in your life that you need to un-mask? Thieves of your joy and peace? Thieves of your clarity and spiritual growth? If you can recognize them, then you can trace them.

Let me remind you of the enemy. Believe it or not, the skill of an evil spirit is to blend in. Think back to snakes—one of their main weapons is camouflage. Evil spirits seek to blend in by placing themselves in atmospheres where it looks like they belong. The enemy often tries to hide himself in the "front lawn" of your deliverance. For example, when you pursue healing, he may try to create offense between you and those who want to help you. He wants you to be turned off by them so you remain stuck. Remember that as Paul and Silas were heading to a place of prayer, they were met by a python spirit. The enemy puts a lot of effort into keeping you from your deliverance.

So, here are five ways to enhance your spiritual awareness.

1. Fast

Fasting strengthens your no—it builds up your ability to resist the enemy's ploys. Fasting exposes where the devil thinks he has a grip. When you fast, the place where your flesh rages is where the enemy is trying to get a hold on you. To enhance your spiritual awareness, you must fast and get your spirit in control.

2. Take heed to internal annoyances

For increased spiritual awareness, you must pay attention to internal annoyances. Notice your spiritual mood when you're in certain places. Don't just dismiss it. This is your spirit's way of saying things like "How long will you let this have access to you?" It's similar to the annoyance Paul felt and can mean that something is not healthy. Something that is affecting your mood might also be affecting your witness and peace. So, take heed to that internal static. That's God's way of saying this is something He wants to cut.

3. Establish devotion

Devotion is about setting aside time to talk with God and hear His voice in return. When you consistently meet with God in prayer, you develop a spiritual ear that recognizes His tone, His cadence, and His heart. This daily communion creates a reference point so that when you need direction, you know immediately whether a voice is God's or not. Think of devotion as spending quality time with your closest friend—the more time you invest, the more intimately you know them. Commit to establishing a daily devotional practice where you can quiet your heart, lift your concerns, and listen for His guidance.

If you don't know God's voice in devotion, you won't know it in direction.

4. Consume the Word

There's a difference between having a head full of scripture and having a heart full of scripture. Knowing a lot of scripture just means you have a good memory. But do you live out those passages? The Bible becomes transformative only when it takes root beyond your intellect and reshapes your desires, decisions, and actions. When God's Word dwells in your heart rather than just in your memory, it becomes a filter through which you interpret your experiences and a lamp that illuminates your path. Make it your aim not just to read the Scripture but also to meditate on it until it becomes part of your spiritual DNA.

5. Be aware of your purpose

The final way to enhance your spiritual awareness is to be aware of your purpose. When you know your purpose, you will be conscious of your assignment and will be watching out for distractions. A lot of us are all over the place because we don't have the anchors of purpose and assignment. When you understand your assignment, you can recognize when something is trying to distract you. But if you don't know what you're supposed to do, you live life aimlessly. And when that happens, everything looks like a target.

My hope is that when you do know your purpose and assignment, you will always remember that the Father has the authority to come and cut whatever He needs to for you to grow. Remember that He's not cutting you to hurt you; He's cutting you to keep you.

QUESTIONS

1. Where in your life might you be misidentifying a spiritual issue as merely a personal problem? How would your response change if you recognized the spiritual dimension?

2. What attachments (like the python spirit) might be constricting your spiritual growth? What steps can you take to allow Jesus to release you from these?

3. How crowded is the microphone of your soul? What voices are competing with the Holy Spirit for your attention?

4. What specific spiritual disciplines can you engage in to enhance your spiritual awareness and discernment?

PRAYER

Dear Father, please help me remember that You have the right to cut every umbilical cord of toxicity and bitterness and whatever else You need to sever so that You can take me to another realm. Bring me to a deeper depth with You. The worst place I can be right now is in the same spot I was this time last year. Lord, cut me so You can keep me. Help me remember that it's not personal; it's spiritual.

Father, please help me also remember that You get joy when I give You glory. I get joy when I recognize that You are orchestrating my steps and when I am not dealing with the repercussions of trying to make something right. That was never Your will. Remind me that You don't just order my steps; You also order my stops. Help me start and continue to grow. Cut whatever You need to cut so I can go wherever You want me to go. In Jesus's name I pray, amen.

BONUS CONTENT

To continue rehabbing your heart, use your smartphone to scan the code for a bonus video diving deeper into the content of this chapter.

URL: waterbrookmultnomah.com/HRChapterSeven

EIGHT

AFTER THE BREAKUP

Then Jesus replied, "Have I not chosen you, the Twelve? Yet one of you is a devil!" (He meant Judas, the son of Simon Iscariot, who, though one of the Twelve, was later to betray him.)

—JOHN 6:70–71

Every one of us has an amazing story God wants to write for us. Yet the stories of our lives—the tales we're telling ourselves or the sagas the enemy has sold to us—can keep us stuck. Even worse, they can keep us broken.

So often, we tell God that we don't trust how He will write our stories. We don't want Him to be the author.

Too many times, Satan uses trauma to bookmark our stories.

If you had a beautiful love story unfolding in your life only to watch it collapse, that doesn't mean your story is over. You still have your kingdom identity. Just because a relationship ends doesn't mean your own story is done. Some of you may need to be reminded that this wasn't the whole book of your life. It's not even the first chapter.

HOW DO WE GRIEVE OVER SOMEBODY
WHO IS STILL ALIVE?

For some of you, that relationship was simply a page. There are many pages left in this chapter of your life, and there are more chapters after this one.

Your story is not over. It's not cut short. There are more pages and chapters left.

So, how do you keep reading? And how do you keep letting God be the author?

In this chapter, I want to help you know how to move on—not just flipping to the next page or the next chapter but going forward in the *right* way.

Why is it such a struggle to move on after a breakup? Maybe it's because you walked away hoping that the person would stop you. You claimed you wanted to move on while deep down waiting for them to hold you back. Now that you are on your own, you can't believe they let you go, and it's left you questioning your worth.

I know all the time and energy and effort I invested. All the finances. All the love.

I know I'm worth more than what they said to me.

It can also be hard to move on because you don't know how to grieve over somebody who's still alive. We have been taught how to mourn when somebody passes away, but how do you grieve when the relationship died but there's no body in the cemetery? The person is very much alive. You might see them at work or sing with them in the choir or pass them on the street or spot them on social media. Maybe you built a life with them and have children with them.

How do you grieve over something that is dead while the person is still alive?

How do you move on in the best way?

I want to help you with that—but through a rather unconventional approach.

Let's start by looking at *you*.

SOMETHING IS WRONG IF YOU'RE NEVER WRONG

It's easy to acknowledge that breakups happen and that some of them are necessary. Some breakups are God's doing, and He often has something better waiting for us. Yes, that's true.

But other breakups are self-induced.

Some of you reading this might want to skip ahead right now, but stay with me. This may be hard to hear, but it's part of the process of conducting a relationship autopsy.

We always like to think that the other person was the problem. That all the red flags were coming from them. But what if I told you the biggest red flag happens when you can't see that you're part of the issue? What if you are the one who keeps sabotaging your relationships? Yes, the breakups hurt, but maybe you are blind to the role you keep playing in your own suffering.

Yes, God loves you, but He also loves your ex.

For some of you, I know that might be hard to read. You might be thinking, *You don't know my ex. How can God love somebody like that?* But God loves both of you.

I know the typical sermon on breakups that can stir people's emotions and get them to shout out. I know the following things I could say to you:

"Yes, they moved on from your life, and they missed out!"

Preach it, Jerry!

"You know what? God is about to take you into a season where some people would wish they had treated you better!"

Amen!

"They might have hurt you behind your back, but God is about to bless you in front of their face!"

Hallelujah!

This is an easy thing to preach and teach and share online. Yes, it will get likes and subscriptions and shares, and it might grow my platform. But here is why I'm not actually saying those things.

I don't want to preach at the expense of a narcissist walking away feeling justified in their behavior. I don't want to teach an emotional message that leaves someone with anger issues feeling justified, like their fits of rage are okay. I can't do that, because bad doctrine gives bad directions and creates bad routes.

I'd rather look at the areas we don't want to face.

Maybe you have a sharp tongue. If so, I'm not going to justify the way you talk. Excuse me, but the problem was your mouth.

What about your control issues? I'm not going to justify the way you act. The problem is your manipulation.

There are two sides of the paradigm when it comes to a breakup.

Yes, sometimes it is God. That's true. God will wreck your plans when He sees that your plans will wreck you. That side of the paradigm is the one often preached and taught.

But what about the other side?

Maybe this breakup was due to you.

Let me share some scriptures to give you a biblical example to consider. John 6:70 says, "Then Jesus replied, 'Have I not chosen you, the Twelve? Yet one of you is a devil!'" The devil He was talking about was Judas, the disciple who would go on to betray Him. Luke 22:47–48 describes this moment:

> While he was still speaking a crowd came up, and the man who was called Judas, one of the Twelve, was leading them. He approached Jesus to kiss him, but

> Jesus asked him, "Judas, are you betraying the Son of
> Man with a kiss?"

Consider this: During Jesus's ministry, while He was doing awesome and wonderful things, the devil was there too. Jesus was preaching while a devil listened nearby. Jesus was eating while a devil was partaking of the same meal. Jesus was on a boat alongside a devil. Jesus was in the same storm the devil was in. Jesus was doing miracles right in front of the devil.

The devil was even sent out by Jesus Himself: "He called the twelve to Himself, and began to send them out two by two, and gave them power over unclean spirits" (Mark 6:7, NKJV).

I wonder whom Jesus paired with Judas?

Judas clearly shows us that saving faith is not the same as religious activity. That's why Jesus tells us in Matthew 7:21–23:

> Not everyone who says to me, "Lord, Lord," will
> enter the kingdom of heaven, but only the one who
> does the will of my Father who is in heaven. Many
> will say to me on that day, "Lord, Lord, did we not
> prophesy in your name and in your name drive out
> demons and in your name perform many miracles?"
> Then I will tell them plainly, "I never knew you. Away
> from me, you evildoers!"

Judas is an example that it's not always others that the enemy uses. Could it be that he has been using you? Don't judge Judas. He betrayed Jesus for thirty pieces of silver, but many of us do it for free! Myself included.

This reminds me of a quote I saw on social media a few years ago. It said that Judas had the best pastor, the best leader, and the best counselor, yet he still betrayed Jesus.

It's not always them. Sometimes it's me.

Of course, God works all things together for the good of those who love Him (Romans 8:28). And yes, this is part of the redemptive story of Christ. A Judas kiss is often the most painful, but it can also be the most purposeful.

Has a breakup changed you because of what that person did to you? Has the hurt made you hurt others because you haven't healed?

I'll be transparent. The first few years of my marriage, I was projecting on my wife, thinking I was protecting her. I warned her about the dangers of serving in ministry. "Ministry is rough," I told her. "You can't trust anybody. You've got to be tough!" But in trying to get her to be tough, I wasn't being tender. I knew that being a pastor is one of the most amazing opportunities you can ever have, but it's also one of the most difficult. I wanted to protect my wife from the reality of pastoring.

You can pray for people and be there when they're going through a crisis, but they can leave after God answers those prayers.

You can eulogize a family's loved ones at their funerals, then never see them again.

People will leave you with calls or emails. That's what happens. People whom you thought were on your team do it. People you served with overseas or men and women you counseled will do it. It happens over and over.

In my mind, I was trying to protect my wife because I was scared that what happened to me would also happen to her.

Because I was afraid of being hurt again, I was hurting her.

Because I was wounded, I was wounding her.

Then God taught me a valuable lesson: *Jerry, you cannot be an effective spiritual doctor if you keep on catching symptoms and viruses from the people you're trying to serve.*

So, yes, sometimes it's others, but other times it's you.

That's why after a breakup it's crucial to perform what I call a relational autopsy. What caused the death of this relationship? Don't just move on. Hold on and wait and ask yourself, *What caused this to die?* Was it a homicide, or was it something God was trying to purify? What ultimately caused the death of your relationship?

Did you kill something?

Did you both murder it together?

Or was God purifying and cleaning your life because He has something greater in store for you?

THE PURSUIT OF UNDERSTANDING IS
PART OF LOVE'S FOUNDATION

It is not easy to realize that you could be part of the problem. As human beings, we have a long history of shifting blame and refusing to take responsibility for the dysfunction in our lives. Remember, however, that you cannot change others; you can only, by the grace of God, change yourself. To progress toward the heart healing God has in store for you, you need to take responsibility for your part in the brokenness you are experiencing in relationships with others. In light of this, here are six symptoms that reveal you're the carrier.

1. You produce junkyards instead of skyscrapers

What do you see when you look back at the relationship? Does it look like rubble?

Are you causing junkyards or building skyscrapers?

Look at your past actions. Did you tear down their confidence? Look at your past words. Did you destroy their self-esteem? Did you tear down or build up? Did your lack of holiness and wholeness contribute to their brokenness?

A whole glass can be used to quench your thirst, but that same glass, if broken, can cut you.

Are you breaking down or building up?

Men, you might say, "I've never laid a hand on a woman!" Just because you don't hurt a woman physically doesn't mean you're not abusive. You might not have laid your hands on her, but you laid your words on her.

For some of you ladies, a lot of brothers have experienced an ample amount of abuse due to your mouths. Girl, you've cut so many bodies with your mouth that you could be called an undertaker! You're trying to destroy him with your words.

Does this sound overly harsh? Let's look at a familiar passage: "Death and life are in the power of the tongue, and those who love it will eat its fruit" (Proverbs 18:21, NKJV).

Your tongue and the words it produces have the power of life and death! So, the quintessential question we each have to ask ourselves is, *What is the condition of my mouth?* Is it a grim reaper or a delivery unit? Is your mouth producing death or birthing life?

If you were a boxing coach, would you be helping the boxer you were training defeat their opponent or crumble to the mat? When I used to box, while I was sparring, my coach would shout instructions.

"Put up your left!" he would say. So, I put up my left hand.

"Watch his right!" So, I made sure to watch my opponent's right hand.

I had a language in my life that helped me know how to fight.

What is the condition of your mouth? Do you produce junkyards or skyscrapers?

2. You're the teacher, never the student

You might be responsible for a breakup if you are a teacher and never a student.

Are you *never* wrong? If so, something is definitely wrong!

The worst combination in the world is when somebody is both arrogant and ignorant. When you are arrogant, you think you know everything, but when you are ignorant, you don't know a thing. That's the worst mixture.

These types of people don't listen when you talk, but then they lay into you when you walk. Even though you were talking, they were never listening to understand. They were just waiting their turn.

Part of the foundation of love is the pursuit of understanding. The basis of long-lasting love—kingdom love—is sacrifice, learning, and unlearning. I have to learn God's definition of love, and I have to unlearn my perception of love.

What does the Bible say love is?

For those of you who are husbands—it is imperative for you to set the tone. Men, you set the tone for love in your household. There is nothing more frustrating to a woman than when her husband is tone-deaf.

Take a moment to stop and listen. Can you hear the chord of heaven? Can you match that key?

Are you always the teacher and never the student? Listen to what Proverbs 26:12 says about this: "Do you see a person wise in their own eyes? There is more hope for a fool than for them."

3. You need to be in control

Maybe the relationship is broken because you have to have control.

Does being with you feel like being in bondage? Does your partner constantly feel like they're undergoing an interrogation process?

A controlling person always needs to know where the other person is and what they're doing. Not because the partner is doing something wrong but because the controlling person is insecure. Not because of the partner's lack of faithfulness but because of the craving to be in charge.

Do you find yourself interrogating others with questions like these? "Where are you going? Who will be there? What are all of you doing?"

If you are driven by a need for control, you always find something wrong with your partner's friends or family. Maybe you rarely hang with them. Even worse, you might try to isolate your partner or spouse. Why? Because you want to be in command.

Maybe you're the issue if you have to have control.

4. You are petty

Maybe the relationship ended because you are petty.

Are you reading this and thinking, *This is not the way I thought this chapter was going to go*? Just hold on—we'll get there in a moment. We will discuss how a problem can be due to God having a bigger and better plan. But we need to acknowledge that sometimes we're the problem. Maybe our attitudes cause bigger issues with God's plan.

So, let me give you a definition. Being petty means giving a calculated comment or response that shows you're holding a record of wrong and throwing it in their face when they're voicing a concern.

You know what pettiness looks like. It's when you turn minor things into major problems. "Why didn't you answer your phone last week when you went out with John?"

Or when you give someone the silent treatment over something trivial. *I'm not gonna say another word to her because I'm so angry.*

It's holding a grudge over something so insignificant. *He didn't take out the trash, so I'm not going to take it out either!*

Pettiness can be nitpicking on purpose, making snarky comments in response to an innocent comment, or bringing up old arguments.

Listen, you cannot expect mature love if you're being childish. Does everything have to go your way? That's childish. What happens when children don't get their way? They throw temper tantrums.

Consider Proverbs 25:21–22: "If your enemy is hungry, give him food to eat; if he is thirsty, give him water to drink. In doing this, you will heap burning coals on his head, and the LORD will reward you." This is the opposite of what our culture tells us to do. Instead of rewarding your flesh by being petty with someone, do good to them. This is the way of Jesus.

You never have to be petty because nobody can reward you like the Lord!

5. You are not faithful

Maybe you were the problem in a failed relationship because you weren't faithful.

Faithfulness is a constant choice. People don't abandon things they want; they abandon things they are using. We have a whole generation that claims they value loyalty when most of us are loyal only to opportunities; we're not loyal to people.

6. You are a liar

Maybe you caused a breakup because you're a liar.

That might feel harsh, but please hear me: One lie—one single lie—can cause a person to question all truths.

Some people have a habit of lying. And they do so for no reason. Then, to make matters worse, they get upset when the person they lie to doesn't believe them!

Things break apart more easily when held together by lies.

It's often not just about the lies, though. Yes, you lied, and you admitted it and asked for forgiveness. But maybe your partner was struggling with something else. It's not that they didn't forgive you for lying. It's the warfare they then must go through every single time you tell them something. They have to wrestle with the question that haunts them:

"Are you really telling me the truth?"

They have to ask that, and every time they do, it frustrates them.

Maybe they can't believe you anymore. Maybe it's the struggle of wondering what to believe and whether to trust. Maybe the problem really was you.

WHAT WE CALL REJECTION MAY BE REDIRECTION FOR RESURRECTION

Let's get to the part most of us want to read about: the other side of examining a breakup. I want to share two passages of Scripture as we consider this.

First let's look at the book of Ruth. At the start, two men from Bethlehem in Judah, named Mahlon and Kilion, went with their parents to live in Moab (1:1–2). The story continues:

> They married Moabite women, one named Orpah and the other Ruth. After they had lived there about ten years, both Mahlon and Kilion . . . died, and Naomi was left without her two sons and her husband. (verses 4–5)

We love to talk about Ruth and Boaz, but we often miss the fact that before Ruth could encounter Boaz, Mahlon had to die. Let's move ahead to when Boaz first approaches Ruth:

Boaz said to Ruth, "My daughter, listen to me. Don't go and glean in another field and don't go away from here. Stay here with the women who work for me. Watch the field where the men are harvesting, and follow along after the women. I have told the men not to lay a hand on you. And whenever you are thirsty, go and get a drink from the water jars the men have filled."

At this, she bowed down with her face to the ground. She asked him, "Why have I found such favor in your eyes that you notice me—a foreigner?"

Boaz replied, "I've been told all about what you have done for your mother-in-law since the death of your husband—how you left your father and mother and your homeland and came to live with a people you did not know before. May the LORD repay you for what you have done. May you be richly rewarded by the LORD, the God of Israel, under whose wings you have come to take refuge." (2:8–12)

Sometimes breakups happen because even though you were so caught up with Mahlon, God truly needs for you to meet Boaz. Think about this: Ruth and Boaz had a son named Obed. And Obed had a son named Jesse. And Jesse had a son named David. Yes, *that* David—King David.

Jesus came through the genealogy of David.

Sometimes that breakup is for a kingdom purpose. The question is, Can you get over your Mahlon?

He was my type. I wanted him. But maybe there is a bigger reason for him not to be there anymore.

She was my type. She always had my back. But maybe there is a bigger purpose for her to no longer be around.

Just because a relationship died doesn't mean something in

you has to die. Many times, what we call rejection is redirection for resurrection!

Did something in you die while you were dating Mahlon? God is redirecting you to resurrect that part of you, to resurrect your joy and your prayer life. Maybe ever since you were dating your Mahlon, you stopped praying. You stopped seeking God's face and studying the Word. You started drinking alcohol. You started messing around.

I'm not talking about legalism here. I'm talking about the downward decline of your faith while you were with your Mahlon.

For some of you wondering why your breakup happened, God has an answer: *Because I have a Boaz for you! I have something better for you!*

Let's look at what Jesus tells His disciples in Matthew 10:11–14:

> Now whatever city or town you enter, inquire who in it is worthy, and stay there till you go out. And when you go into a household, greet it. If the household is worthy, let your peace come upon it. But if it is not worthy, let your peace return to you. And whoever will not receive you nor hear your words, when you depart from that house or city, shake off the dust from your feet. (NKJV)

What does Jesus tell us to do? "Let your peace return to you." Do you want to get your peace back?

If you and your Mahlon or Emma or James didn't work out, let your peace come back to you. Jesus is telling us to not leave our peace back there. Don't leave your peace in a past relationship, a previous year, or a former relationship.

I need you to learn how to brush that off. Shake off the dust from your feet.

In this biblical snapshot, Jesus is sharing one of the methods for you to be healthy as you move on to the next village—the next relationship or opportunity: You have to shake off the dust of Mahlon, of what happened.

"But, Pastor J, you don't know what they did to me!"

You are right. I don't. But I do know what bitterness will do to you! Bitterness only contaminates the container. I don't know what they did to you, but I do know how a calloused heart will affect you.

In this passage, Jesus shows us three things that will help us in the aftermath of a breakup. First, staying in a place where you're not received is wasting your time, and wasting time prolongs what is really yours. What is really yours? Boaz, not Mahlon. You can be a whole package, but if you end up at the wrong address, the receiver will mishandle you. So, Jesus tells us not to stay in a place where we're not received. Shake that off.

Second, we can learn from this passage that God always gives us shake-it-off space. You remove the dust from one village before you go to the next one. If you don't shake off what happened with Mahlon, you'll take it with you. If you don't shake off what happened with your ex or with that church hurt, you will end up taking old dirt into a new season. Whoever you are with now will feel like you're being dusty. You will look dusty. Maybe you're dusty because you haven't addressed the sand of a former village. The residue of what you went through is still on you.

Third, Jesus challenges us to take our peace with us. If it didn't work with Mahlon, there must be a Boaz. If they didn't receive you in that village, there must be another village that will.

We can't highlight this part of the chapter while ignoring the previous section. So, start with yourself. *Am I the one that is contributing to hurting others?*

Because remember—it's not always them. Sometimes it's you.

But other times, it was them. And if that's what happened, then God is trying to show you something.

I have more for you.

DISCOVERING DESTINY AND PURPOSE
EXPEDITES HEALING

Let me end this chapter with some hard truths. Maybe it has already been full of some hard truths for you, but here is some advice I wish I had gotten earlier.

So, a breakup happened. Maybe they were responsible, or maybe it was you. Most likely you are both responsible on some level. The best thing you can do now is own your part and learn from it. Regardless, they are no longer in your life. Here are some hard truths to then acknowledge and accept:

1. You will miss them

Yes, you will miss that person. You will think about them. But missing them is not permission to return. Missing them doesn't mean you're in your flesh. It's natural.

On cold nights and certain holidays, you will miss them.

In unexpected moments, you will miss them.

That's the crazy thing about healing—it's a messy process. One day you'll be fine, and the next day you'll be crying your eyes out. That doesn't mean you're crazy. It means you are human. It means you have needs.

You're learning how to grieve over what's still alive.

You will miss them, but that's not a permission slip to return. God never cracks open the Red Sea so that you can return to the past. He only parts seas so that you can depart and move forward.

2. You have mutual friends

The second hard truth about a breakup is that you will have mutual friends. Don't make them choose sides. Your breakup was with one person, not with everybody else. So don't put your friends through the same thing you're going through.

Remember, this is something God might be preparing you for. Boaz might be waiting in another village, so don't blame other people when it wasn't their fault. This is more about what God is doing with *you*.

3. You will get angry

It is not that you *might* get angry. You *will* get angry once you start missing them and after you have to deal with your mutual friends. You will get angry at times, but that's okay. Be angry. Grieve properly. Being angry is a part of it.

Be angry over all the time that went by and that you can't get back.

Be angry over the lies they told you and the lack of love they showed you.

It's okay for you to get angry. The Bible literally says this in Ephesians 4:26: "'Be angry, and do not sin': do not let the sun go down on your wrath" (NKJV). But don't allow what is just supposed to be a state to become a season. You can be upset, but understand that either God caused the breakup to send you to something better or you did this. And if it's something you did, then you need to get healing and embrace the season of shaking it off so you don't continue this pattern.

Remember, God loves you just like He loves them. So even if you were the one that caused it, God still has good things in store for you.

4. You will have to throw some things away

Here is a very practical but real truth: There are some things you're going to have to throw away. Maybe it's a piece of clothing or a small artifact. Or maybe it's something bigger, like social media.

Social media can be a major trigger when we haven't healed. Let's be honest: For many of us, social media is a scab picker. We're trying to heal, but every time we get on Instagram or Facebook or TikTok, we see our ex, and it's like we are picking at our own skin.

When do you know you're healed? You are healed when you see the person who cut you and you don't want to cut them back. But make sure to throw away things that keep on picking at your scabs.

5. Do a relational autopsy

I've already talked about this, but I'll say it again: Do an autopsy and ask yourself why the relationship died. Understanding the cause of death is crucial for healing.

I want you to get to a place where you no longer question your value if your Mahlon dies or a relationship ends. God needs you to understand that you're infinitely valuable.

Your value is so great that perhaps God is reserving you for where He's sending you. Or maybe God is saying, *I need to deal with this in you.*

A relationship won't fix a problem inside you. It will not heal your wounds. The end of this relationship is likely an invitation from God to change and grow.

Examine why a relationship died, and deal with truth behind it.

6. Discovered destiny and purpose expedite healing

After I got saved, when I was in college studying to be a student pastor, I broke up with my girlfriend because she didn't want to be a pastor's wife. I feel that the Lord helped me heal faster because it ultimately would not have been a good marriage. That relationship wouldn't have served my purpose.

You heal faster when you're doing what you were created to do. And this leads me into the seventh hard truth.

7. Pursue destiny

Pursue your destiny. When you understand what you're called to do, it helps you heal, because you recognize that the relationship was totally out of purpose. You can see that it wouldn't have worked for what God is calling you to do, for the ministry you are trying to do.

There were reasons for the breakup. Looking at those reasons is not the easiest thing to do, but it's necessary for us to continue to move toward our destiny and purpose. God might be needing to work out something inside you, or He might be protecting you for something bigger and better.

God gives us strength to move on. Take His strength with you. Take His peace with you, and don't leave it in a relationship that happened years ago. But don't just move on. Give God the glory, and magnify Him. Move on in the right way. Move on with health and with humility, leaning into the lessons He is teaching you amid all the change. Move on to that beautiful place God has planned for you.

QUESTIONS

1. Have you conducted a relationship autopsy on past failed relationships? (Think about friendships, parents, and siblings too, not just romantic relationships.) What patterns do you see that might be contributing to these breakups?

2. In what ways might you be contributing to relationship problems? How open are you to examining your own behaviors rather than focusing solely on others' faults?

3. How have you been grieving over someone who is still alive? What steps can you take to properly process this grief and move forward?

4. What might God be trying to protect you from or direct you toward through a painful breakup? How can you embrace this new direction?

PRAYER

Dear Heavenly Father, help me understand that Your will for my life is better than my will. Help me, God, to be able to heal and move on—not just for the sake of moving on but with health. Help me move on in the right way and with clarity so that I don't heal crooked but can operate in wholeness. I pray that You will move in these words. Help me see that learning about healing means absolutely nothing if You aren't magnified and glorified. Help me learn how to grieve over somebody who is still alive. And help me heal from past hurts, whether caused by others or self-inflicted. Thank You for the Boaz You have in store for me. In Jesus's name I pray, amen.

BONUS CONTENT

To continue rehabbing your heart, use your smartphone to scan the code for a bonus video diving deeper into the content of this chapter.

URL: waterbrookmultnomah.com/HRChapterEight

NINE

RED FLAGS ARE WARNINGS, NOT INVITATIONS

> They went to Phrygia, and then on through the region of
> Galatia. Their plan was to turn west into Asia province, but the
> Holy Spirit blocked that route.
>
> —ACTS 16:6 (MSG)

What is God's will for your life? God has a personal will for you in the same way He has one for me, and it's all under the umbrella of giving Him glory. In this chapter, I want to focus on God's will for each of us and how to know when something is or is not His will.

Let me share four ways we can know when something is God's will: It's what you're gifted to do, what you're passionate to do, what you're graced to do, or what you're paid to do. Some people think that if they're not paid to do something, then it must not be God's will, but that's not necessarily true. You can be passionate about something that doesn't earn an income to pay your bills. All your gifts are for God's glory.

YOU WANNA CHANGE? WELL, JESUS IS THE CASHIER

I can preach, speak, do poetry, and rap, and I use all of those for the glory of God. The one I'm most graced for is preaching. How do you know whether you're graced for something? It is easy and natural for you. When I open the Bible, God just floods information to me. Trying to rap, though, is a little harder. Now don't get me wrong—I can flow. J-Flo. I can flow. That's one of my gifts. Here's a sample:

Jesus took my place; Heaven's now my home.

Your boy is off the hook. You hear the dial tone?

My signal's real strong; my volume's on high.

I'm on a family plan. I share lines with my God, ya.

In Christ I'm so secure and Jesus is the cure.

Because He can clean you from your wickedness and make
    you pure.

Just have ears to hear and keep the Lord near.

You wanna change? Well, Jesus is the cashier.

Putting that together took time for me. Rap is not my primary gift, and I know that because it's not easy for me. It's easy for somebody like Lecrae or KB.

So, how do you identify your primary gift? What is the easiest thing for you to do? That is your graced ability.

Again, being passionate about something doesn't always mean you're going to get paid for it. My wife was passionate about worship, but she was a teacher for fourteen years. Being passionate about worship was not paying our bills; her gifts as an elementary teacher were. So don't let people tell you, "If you're passionate about something, you should get paid for it." Maybe or maybe not. Regardless, we should use all those gifts for God's glory.

So, how do you know something is God's will? First, there is favor. Second, there's fruit—undeniable evidence that this is growing. If you say you're called to teach but nobody's coming to your class, then you have to consider that teaching may not be God's will. Third, it complements God's Word. If it contradicts His Word, then it's not His will. And fourth is what I already mentioned—it's something you are graced to do, something that comes easily.

How do you know something is *not* God's will? I will address that in more detail later. Just know that when God has graced you to do something, He will give you favor and there will be fruit.

DON'T MISS GOD'S WILL FOR YOUR LIFE

One of the greatest challenges I see for this generation is that we don't know how to focus on our own lanes. We have an overexposure to everybody else's world, so when we are constantly scrolling and seeing all these other people's lives, it can cause us to underappreciate where God has us.

To be honest, not knowing how everybody else is doing could be for our benefit!

When I was in high school, there was a sophomore named Reggie who got a new car. Our school did not allow students to leave campus for lunch whether they had cars or not. But this kid drove to Sonic for lunch anyway. When he pulled into the parking lot, a cop was standing outside and walked up to him. Reggie was terrified as the police officer started to write a ticket.

"Please don't give me a ticket!" Reggie pleaded. "Please don't! I'm sorry—I won't do it again."

"Go ahead and get to class," the cop said, letting him off with just a warning.

The next day, one of Reggie's friends, Bryson, decided to accompany him. *He got away with it, so I might as well go with him too,* he reasoned. So, Reggie drove to Sonic again. But this time when he saw the cop sitting there in his car, Reggie wasn't as scared.

When the policeman came up to his window, Reggie stated his case. "I'm sorry, officer. I just wanted to show my friend my new car. So, I took him to have some lunch."

The officer let both students go.

The very next day, Reggie and Bryson went back to Sonic, and once again they found the police officer sitting in his car in the parking lot. Reggie drove up beside the cop, but as he rolled down his window, he could see the policeman writing a ticket.

"Come on, Officer Neil," Reggie said, "I thought you were cool! This is not fair."

Officer Neil answered, "Oh, you want fair?" He kept writing for several moments, then handed Reggie three tickets. "Here you go," he said. "One, two, three. And here are three tickets for your friend."

This little story illustrates what we do too often when it comes to God's will. We mistake God's grace as a permission slip for getting by. Just like Bryson, when we go along for the ride for something that is not God's will for our lives, we will get the same ticket as the driver!

I post my teachings and sermons online regularly because I'm passionate about helping people know God's will. I don't want any of us to experience a storm that is not profitable for our lives. If you're going to experience pain, it should be purposeful and not just because you're living outside the will of God. You and I can make mistakes on many things and get a lot of things wrong. But you do not want to mistake God's will for your life and your eternal placement! That is why I'm so passionate about the lessons in this book.

I want to always be a brother, a servant, a husband, a father, a leader, a pastor, and an author who tells you the truth at the expense of hurting your feelings but causes your spirit to grow. Why? I'll repeat what I said in the last chapter:

Bad doctrine gives bad directions.

And bad directions cause us to take wrong routes.

Wrong routes then cause us to encounter wrong people and wrong places that are not profitable for our assignments or callings.

I used to wonder why so many people choose the hard road in life. But then I got this revelation and epiphany from God. Due to bad teaching and our pride, we see only one route, not two. We don't see broad and narrow; we see only broad.

I want to help you discern the difference between thinking a decision is right because it's what you want and making the right decision because it's what God wants for you. We need to know how to make holistic choices that complement not our own wills but the will of God for our lives.

WE MAY WANT THE REWARDING BUT OVERLOOK THE WARNING

With so many preaching and teaching on the will of God, we have an embarrassing amount of information on it. Endless sermons and podcasts and books rightly tell us that the safest place to be is in the will of God. But how do you know God's will for your life? How do you identify God's hand on a thing instead of your own? How can you discern His will versus your own?

One way God lets us know that something is not His will is through warnings. He cautions us. He shows us red flags. But here's the hard thing: It'll be tough for you to see the spiritual red flags when you have already decided what you want God to say!

It'll be difficult to discern the will of God because it's something you want.

So, how do you identify the warnings of God? Let's look at Acts 16:6–8 in *The Message*:

> They went to Phrygia, and then on through the region of Galatia. Their plan was to turn west into Asia province, but the Holy Spirit blocked that route. So they went to Mysia and tried to go north to Bithynia, but the Spirit of Jesus wouldn't let them go there either. Proceeding on through Mysia, they went down to the seaport Troas.

Look at these two words: "their plan." Paul and Timothy's plan was to turn west. We all make plans, right? A plan to marry that person, to start that business or ministry, to move to this place. In Paul and Timothy's case, the Holy Spirit blocked them— not once but twice. God was telling them, *My will is not here, and My will is not there. Paul, I need you to go on through Mysia.*

How many times does the Holy Spirit block us? Yet when things don't work out for us, we tend to take matters into our own hands or find our own reasons:

I've got to grind harder. I've got to pray more. I've got to keep pushing.

This is just bad weather.

This is the devil doing this.

Can you identify the blocking of the Holy Spirit? Yes, your block game is strong, but so is the Holy Spirit's! We will block people in a heartbeat. So will the Holy Spirit if something is going to get in the way of God's will for your life and your calling.

I think as pastors we have done the body a huge disservice

because we preach so much about the rewarding of God. How many messages are full of "blessings" and "your season" and "your time" and "abundance" and "prosperity"? We have done damage to the Christian body because we overpreach the rewarding of God but underpreach the warnings of God. In actuality, it's the warnings of God that position us to experience the rewarding of God!

Many of us want the reward without the obedience.

We want the rewarding but overlook the warning.

So many people are suffering and dealing with pain because they don't know how to identify when God is saying *This is not Me* versus *This is Me.* They're seeing red flags not as warnings but as invitations.

Your emotional and relational intelligence matters because decisions are potters. They mold you. They mold the way you see God and others. They mold the way you see your pastors and your parents. Decisions sculpt you.

Whenever we're wounded, we mainly create patterns of defending ourselves and our insecurities and fears. It's so easy to rationalize our way out of dealing with our emotions and past wounds.

"The Bible says for us to guard our hearts," you might say. "That's what I'm doing!"

But some of you are not guarding your hearts. You've walled them in. Your hearts are in prison, and healing can't get through.

"I just don't do people," you say.

But the truth is, you have a fear of repeated pain.

You can't refuse to talk about pain and call that healing. God won't fill a void that you avoid.

Maybe you have a history of pain, a story of abuse and trauma.

Maybe your history is so full of betrayal that it causes you to push people away. Yes, you want to love them, but your pain and paranoia won't let you because your heart is imprisoned. This causes you to stay stuck in a place outside of God's will. You stay frustrated with Him.

You wonder why God isn't breathing on your behalf.

You wonder why God isn't blessing your ministry, building your business, or brightening your situation.

You forget what He has told us. *I will not bless what I am not authoring.*

I want everybody who says "I'm cool" and "I'm good" to understand this: Whatever you don't deal with in this season will show up in the front row of your heart and your emotions in the next season.

We need to understand that God has a preferred will for each of us. Scripture tells us this. Micah 6:8 says, "He has shown you, O mortal, what is good. And what does the LORD require of you? To act justly and to love mercy and to walk humbly with your God." And Acts 3:19 states, "Repent, then, and turn to God, so that your sins may be wiped out, that times of refreshing may come from the Lord."

God has a preferred will for your life. He has a preferred will for your children, your home, and your ministry. But we must become people who are spiritually educated enough to identify God's will from ours. Until we can see His warnings and differentiate our desires from His, we will constantly stay in a season called *stuck*.

WRITE YOUR PURPOSE IN PERMANENT MARKER BUT YOUR STEPS IN PENCIL

Each chapter in this book so far has shown places where we might be seeing red flags as invitations instead of warnings. We might not be seeing God's will in our lives because of the different topics we've already covered, so let's review them.

Problematic patterns

If you feel that God doesn't hear you, is the problem your routine? Maybe you are not sticking with the routine of coming to church. Perhaps you're mad at someone and need to forgive them, but ultimately the problem is your pattern of entertaining a person like that in the first place. You have a routine of welcoming toxicity into your life. The problem in your life is the pattern and the routine. This can prevent you from knowing God's will.

God wants us to expose our negative patterns. That means we have to find them. Finding a problem is like cutting a twig or plucking up a root. And this is why I know without a shadow of a doubt that God wants us to do therapy. It's why I feel called to do Therapy Thursdays week after week. Sunday is not enough. And for some, Sunday and Therapy Thursday are not enough—they need professional therapy as well. There are patterns in our lives that get in the way of our intimacy with God.

Christians are supposed to be mirrors of Christ, but some of us need healing before we reflect God in the earth. Too many of our mirrors have no reflection. God wants us to be light, not shade. He wants us to be salt, not sugar. He wants us to be fruitful, not barren. But our patterns can get in the way of that. That's why we have to expose them! And therapy can be the thing that unearths these patterns.

Seeing our true selves

We should never forget that our Heavenly Father made us and that He makes no mistakes.

We need to remember that He called us, even though He knew all the stupid stuff we would do.

We must remember to have the right perspective about ourselves—to see ourselves as God sees us. When He created us, He said it was good. That means we need to value what God values. Loving ourselves the right way means not thinking more highly of ourselves than we ought to think. It means choosing to believe and to think the same thoughts that the Most High does about us.

When you know the you God created you to be, then you have purpose. I've said this many times: Purpose is a fixer. Purpose fixes problems. So, a successful life means you've fixed whatever problem you were purposed to fix.

Childhood trauma

One reason the enemy uses trauma is to contaminate our concentration. Untreated pain from our past causes a mismanagement of our focus. And there is nothing more exhausting to the soul than mismanaged effort.

Remember that untreated childhood trauma can blur our discernment. Not addressing the wounds from our past can cause us to not hear God clearly. We're hearing our own pain instead of God's will. That causes a desire to do what we want instead of what God wants.

But God is so good, because He always flips what the enemy has planned for evil into something good. God turns our trauma into a triumph for Him. Yes, you went through a mess, but that was just so you could meet the Messiah. God is going to clean you of your mess and make you a trauma breaker. To break free of trauma and dysfunction, though, we have to hear God's voice and learn His will for our lives.

Crowded minds

Our minds are so crowded with worry and what-ifs that it can be impossible to hear a single word from God. God becomes just another thing in the long line of our overthinking.

We often forget that God sees our struggles and hears our prayers. He desires to help us, but we must trust Him during the difficult process of change. This requires us to be able to hear Him and know how He wants to help us.

Worst-case scenarios

The safest place to be is in the will of God. Safety is provided not by bricks or your rottweiler or your 9mm but by God's will. Too often, however, we allow our fears to get in the way of His will.

Mental conjuring of the worst-case scenario can cause our blessing to be stuck in transit. How many more times will we allow our own negative thinking to play a role in our suffering? Culture can cultivate pessimism. It's the pessimist who complains about the rain and fears it's going to flood, while the optimist knows that every storm cloud eventually runs out of rain. The realist has an evacuation plan. But the kingdom thinker knows that all things work together for good to them who love God.

Whether the sun is shining or it's raining, all things will work together.

If there is a storm and it floods, all things will work together.

Whether I'm hired or fired, all things will work together.

In a recession or a pandemic, all things will work together.

On the mountaintop or in the valley, all things will work together.

In my singleness or in my marriage, all things will work together.

The kingdom thinker remembers that our God is sovereign and that the outcome belongs to Him. The kingdom thinker will be able to hear from Him.

Control issues

Remember, control issues are our attempt to traffic in sovereignty.

Proverbs 16:9 says, "In their hearts humans plan their course, but the LORD establishes their steps." Verse 33 says, "The lot is cast into the lap, but its every decision is from the LORD." And Proverbs 19:21 tells us the exact same thing but in a different way: "Many are the plans in a person's heart, but it is the LORD's purpose that prevails."

So, what about your plans? Do you know what God is planning for your life? God has a purpose for you, and that purpose is going to prevail over your plans!

How do we lower our anxiety? By seeking God for His plan and purpose. That way, we won't disappoint Him because of all our plans. God is reminding us in these verses that He is running this.

You can write your purpose in permanent marker, but you'd better write your steps in pencil!

It's not personal; it's spiritual

Discerning God's voice when we're in the middle of conflicting influences is crucial for our spiritual growth. But how do we hear God's voice over our own and other voices?

Hearing requires proximity, and proximity determines temperature.

Somebody who is cold in their faith is someone who is far from the Son. Think of that person as a Pluto Christian. I know that Pluto isn't considered a planet anymore, but the reason it is so frigid is because it's so far away from the sun. And the reason Venus is so hot is that it's in proximity to the sun. In the same way, somebody who's on fire for the things of God is someone who's close to the Son.

Maybe you can't recognize the voice of God because of your distance from Him.

Look at the word *recognition*. It is re-cognition. *Cognition* is "acquiring knowledge and understanding through thought, experience, and the senses."[1] And *re-* means "again."[2] So, I'm speaking right now to your cognitive self. When you see somebody who looks familiar, you don't say, "I cognize them." No, you say, "I recognize them." You can't recognize me if you haven't encountered me in the first place. You can't recognize my voice if you haven't heard it.

Again, hearing requires proximity, and proximity determines temperature. Your encounters are tied to your recognition. If there is no intentional encounter, there is no recognition. So, the more you deliberately spend time with God, the easier it will be to recognize when God is speaking, because you're not seeking Him only when you need Him. You're seeking Him out of intentionality.

Stuck

Sometimes we're unable to know God's will because we're in that place where none of us wants to be: *stuck.*

1. *Oxford Dictionary of English,* 3rd ed. (2010), under "cognition."
2. *Merriam-Webster,* "re-," merriam-webster.com/dictionary/re-.

Do you ever feel like you don't sense God's presence anymore? That you're not going anywhere?

I believe the Lord gave me an acronym for this. Anytime you feel *stuck,* can it be because you're *s*till *t*rying *u*ngodly *c*onnections *k*nowingly?

Maybe you're stuck not because God isn't answering your prayers but because you're not being obedient. Perhaps you're not hearing God's will for your life because you're keeping yourself from moving forward.

GOD CONTROLS THE RAIN, BUT WE MIGHT CREATE SPRINKLERS

If we were to be honest, all of us have times when God shows us red flags yet we view them like invitations. We try to make things work because it's what we want. We can be narcissistic and try to manipulate situations. We do things our way instead of God's.

So, how do we identify something that is not the will of God? Let me give you five ways:

Uneasiness or the lack of peace

The biggest red flag God can ever give us is the lack of His peace. You may be looking for God to tell you whether or not something is His will when He's already answered you by the lack of peace in your heart. Something is off inside you. You know something is not right. You have a sense of unease in your soul. You feel it in your gut, but you're deliberately choosing not to face those feelings. Those of us who are believers have the presence of the Holy Spirit dwelling inside us, and He will give us those feelings in our guts. The Holy Spirit will let us know that something is not God's will by giving us an uneasiness or a lack of peace.

Blocks or a lack of fruit

Another way God reveals that something is not His will is by blocking us or not yielding fruit. We read about a blockage from God earlier in Acts 16, when the Holy Spirit diverted Paul and Timothy's route. If we encounter resistance and restraint, that may be God saying, *This is not Me*. We need to understand that we can't go that way.

A lack of fruit happens when you're trying to push for something but it is simply not growing. God controls the rain, but a lot of times we create sprinklers. Even though there is no fruit to be seen, we're trying to grow it ourselves! If we haven't identified that this is not something God wants us to do, we attempt to do it on our own, but it still produces no fruit. Fruit is the evidence we need that God's hand is on our efforts.

We shouldn't simply hope for the fruit—we need to *see* the fruit. So, make sure to recognize when God is blocking your path or when there is no fruit.

Vessels

The third way God lets us know that something is not His will is through vessels, or people. This is for all of you who say you don't need to go to church. God can choose to speak to you through lots of different people—your spouse, a friend, a therapist. How did God communicate to His people in the Old Testament? Through His prophets.

Jeremiah 3:15 says, "I will give you pastors according to mine heart, which shall feed you with knowledge and understanding" (KJV). It doesn't say that you will be fed with entertainment or colloquialisms. You won't be fed to make you shout like you've lost your mind. No, you will be fed with knowledge and understanding.

One thing I pride myself on is wanting all of us to be learned people, knowledgeable people, so that nobody can talk us out of our faith. But I can't feed somebody with knowledge unless they listen. I also need somebody to instruct me, because wisdom is the best teacher.

Sometimes God wants you to just learn through the situation or season you are facing. And we learn through vessels.

Close calls

We can know that something is not God's will when we experience those close calls—the "almosts"—in life. Maybe you almost fell into something but caught yourself in time. It was a close call. You almost made the mistake of doing that thing, and it ended up being a close call. You got scared when your cycle was late—close call. Many times, that is God saying, *I'm blocking this route.* We experience a small indicator of what's behind a closed door so we avoid opening it.

Third-party observations

The fifth way we can know whether something is not God's will is through third-party observations. In other words, we see what happens to someone else and decide we don't want to reap the same results they did. We can see it happen right in front of us. It's a script we read too many times.

Proverbs 27:12 says, "The prudent see danger and take refuge, but the simple keep going and pay the penalty." Don't pay for something with your peace because you want God to bless what He is not offering.

IT LIGHTS ALL MYSTERIOUS PATHS

One last gentle reminder. So often, we fail to hear God's voice or understand His will because we are not reading the Bible. Or as I like to say, the lamp of our Bible reading isn't lit. If you use the lamp of your Bible reading and stay in devotion, you will know when something is not God's will. Staying in God's Word will reveal false doctrine or people to look out for. This is why the psalmist says in Psalm 119:105, "Thy word is a lamp unto my feet, and a light unto my path" (KJV).

It is hard to see God's will in your life if your Bible is dusty or if you open it only when your pastor tells you to turn to Genesis 40. Don't fall into the trap of using your lamp only when you're trying to recover from a breakup or when you want God to give you something. If you live with the lamp of the Word lit as you walk through life, you can see God's will.

There's an acronym for *lamp* that I want to leave with you: It *lights all mysterious paths*. Isn't that good? Remember, John 1:14 says, "The Word [Jesus] became flesh." So, when we have intimacy with Jesus and when we stay in the Bible, the Word lights all our mysterious paths.

QUESTIONS

1. What red flags have you ignored in the past that you now recognize as God's warnings? What were the consequences?

2. Where in your life right now might God be showing you red flags? How are you responding to these warnings?

3. How can you better distinguish God's will from your own desires? What spiritual practices might help you recognize His voice more clearly?

4. What steps can you take to write your purpose in permanent marker while keeping your specific steps in pencil?

PRAYER

Dear Father, please help me learn and get the wisdom necessary so I can be in Your will versus upset at You because of my will. I know it is Your will for me to experience rewards from You, but I recognize that they come when I obey You. I acknowledge that I may be frustrated at not experiencing the blessings the Bible speaks about because I am not following Christ the way I'm told to. Give me the wisdom and guidance to know and submit to Your will and enjoy Your will forever. Help me be someone who loves You and who is fully submitted to Your will so that I can glorify You. I know You have a preferred will for my life. I give You all the praise and all the honor. In Jesus's name, amen.

BONUS CONTENT

To continue rehabbing your heart, use your smartphone to scan the code for a bonus video diving deeper into the content of this chapter.

URL: waterbrookmultnomah.com/HRChapterNine

TEN

I DON'T WANT TO BE LIKE THIS

Love the Lord your God with all your heart and with all your soul and with all your mind and with all your strength.

—MARK 12:30

When you first started reading this book, maybe you were thinking the opening words of the introduction and the title of this chapter:

I don't want to be like this.

My hope is that the past nine chapters have given you some steps for how to allow the Holy Spirit to change your heart. I pray that you have discovered new ways to look at your mind and have found tools to battle issues related to it. But what I hope the most as you finish this book is that you not only *learned* a lot but also have *experienced* a lot. Far be it for us to have heads that are full of the Bible but hearts that are empty of change.

Over the years, this is one reason I have seen people walk away from the faith. They keep talking about a reality they have never experienced. They might be good at quoting scriptural truth and posting it, sharing it, and podcasting it, but experiencing it? Truly experiencing the peace of God? Experiencing healing? Transformation? That's totally different from saying, "God will set you free." That's totally different from quoting, "Be transformed by the renewing of your mind." What we want is to be able to say the following words:

"No, I've been there, and now I'm here."

The Word works, but we have to work it.

STOP MEASURING YOUR STRENGTH BY HOW MUCH YOU CAN TAKE

My hope is that you haven't just read or heard these words but that you have experienced them. That you are currently working on them like I am.

I know that many of you truly carry the scars of trauma with you, so a lot of this is surely difficult. Experiencing this—working on this—is a lot easier said than done. I understand, and I definitely don't want to be insensitive. So, let me encourage you:

You did the best that you could. And right now, you're trying to do the best that you can.

Yes, you were only a child when that happened. Yes, it was unfair. You didn't know they were going to take advantage of you like that. Maybe this is all you've ever seen. But please hear me out:

We don't have to keep everything we've inherited!

Perhaps those past wounds didn't just make you tough. Maybe they made you a version of yourself that contradicts the version God needs you to be to fulfill your assignment. Stop measuring your strength by how much you can take.

That didn't make you tough—it made you hard.

That didn't make you stronger—it made you bitter.

They didn't increase your discernment—they increased your suspicion.

So, now after all that, most of your smiles traffic in fraudulence instead of being truly authentic.

All of us, especially those of us in the church, need wisdom to know the difference between when God is using something to develop us and when something is not from God. Because truthfully, sometimes you're tolerating a person or issue He never sent. We need wisdom in this area so we can stop confusing what God is using to develop our character with what we're choosing to tolerate.

I praise God for all my brothers and sisters who recognize unhealthy patterns and take action. I am thankful the Holy Spirit has convinced you of things that are not bringing you closer to Him, that are not conducive to molding and shaping you into the image and likeness of Jesus. Praise God that He's revealed unhealthy patterns to us! But please hear me:

It's one thing to end something that's unhealthy, but it's a whole nother thing to end the unhealthy version of yourself that allowed it and liked it. See the difference?

I stopped doing that because it was unhealthy.

God transformed my heart, so I no longer allow unhealthy things in my life.

These are two totally different concepts.

Others can offer you guidance, and I can give you counsel. The Holy Spirit will also give you counsel, conviction, and comfort. But only you can work on your consistency. It's *your* responsibility to do the work.

But I know that even as the Word of the Lord is going forth, your pain is going forth too. So, you might be working as hard as you can, yet you still can't hear from God.

There is a version of you that is needed as a believer to carry out God's commands:

The *loving-me* version.

This is a command in John 13:35: "By this everyone will know that you are my disciples, if you love one another."

When I began my journey of really starting to think God's thoughts about myself and trying to have a biblical perspective of Jerry, these truths came like a curveball I never saw coming. This journey included ending the verbal abuse toward myself and taking every thought captive. It included looking through the Scriptures and seeing myself not as an object of wrath but as a student of the Word, a minister of the gospel. Even though God knew how jacked up I was, He still called me. I learned not to use grace as a permission slip to engage in sin but to live a life of obedience and repentance due to what God has said about me and all the blessings He desires to give. These aren't the sort of blessings we normally think of, like houses and cars, or the kind that most prosperity speakers will promise you to make you shout. These are the blessings God desires to fill me with because I hunger and thirst after His Word.

There's a version of you that is needed for you to carry out God's command. Let's examine that command and how you can live it out.

Love God. Love you. Love them.

LOVE GOD. LOVE YOU. LOVE THEM.

In Mark 12, some religious leaders approached Jesus in the temple and asked questions they hoped would trap Him. They wanted Jesus to say something that would get Him arrested. Let's pick the story up in verses 28–31:

> One of the teachers of the law came and heard them debating. Noticing that Jesus had given them a good

answer, he asked him, "Of all the commandments, which is the most important?"

"The most important one," answered Jesus," is this: 'Hear, O Israel: The Lord our God, the Lord is one. Love the Lord your God with all your heart and with all your soul and with all your mind and with all your strength.' The second is this: 'Love your neighbor as yourself.' There is no commandment greater than these."

There are five words in this passage that I breezed by for many years: "Love your neighbor as yourself."

Who is your neighbor? Anybody in proximity to you. The one person ahead of you in line at Walmart is your neighbor. The guy who cut you off in traffic is your neighbor. These are your neighbors—people God calls you to love as yourself.

There is a kingdom order to these commandments that matters. The following chart will show this. The kingdom order is to love God, love you, and love them. Why is that sequence important? Because when I love God, that will cause me to love what God loves. And what does God love? He loves me. So, it's Godlike for me to love what God loves.

| LOVE GOD | > | LOVE YOU | > | LOVE THEM |

Loving God with all your heart and soul and mind and strength means you love His Word. You love being committed to Him, having fellowship with Him, and experiencing intimacy with Him. All of that will begin affecting your personality. When you love the

Lord and these things start to happen, you will also start to love yourself. And now everybody you encounter experiences the love you have for God and the love God has for you. Your neighbors are getting the overflow of your love for God and for yourself.

The order matters: Love God. Love you. Love them.

There is a second chart I want you see. It's possible you have this order mixed up. You might have them first, but they have you last. If you love them first and you second, the way you view love for you is based on the way they love you.

$$\text{LOVE THEM} > \text{LOVE YOU} > \text{LOVE GOD}$$

Heartbreak is imminent when we exaggerate our place in somebody else's heart!

Do you think that where you have them is the same place they have you? That is not true. Loving them first will always cause your love to be predicated on the way they view you and approve of you. And it will also cause you to always put God last.

The third chart shows what happens if you love yourself first. This is what our culture teaches us to do, and when you do this, you become arrogant, prideful, and self-dependent. When you say, "I'm self-made," everything in life becomes about you. And notice—God is last here as well. We put God last and then expect Him to respond first to our every request!

$$\text{LOVE YOU} > \text{LOVE THEM} > \text{LOVE GOD}$$

IT'S HARD TO EXTEND LOVE WHEN
OUR HEARTS ARE BANKRUPT

How do we go from lesser versions of us to the versions God requires us to be? We ask our Father to teach us how to love what
He loves. And for starters, that means He loves us.

How many of us really love what God loves?

Do you truly love yourself the way God loves you?

Maybe you're struggling as you read or listen to this. You
might think there is no way to even *begin* loving yourself the way
God loves you. Yes, you love God, but you're not pursuing a life
of obedience and surrender. You're not pursuing a life of becoming the version of you that God called you to be.

Maybe you're stuck in childhood trauma.

Perhaps you can't help but feel bitter and resentful about the
way things have gone in your life.

Maybe you get headaches and your chest feels tight.

All of this is due to everything you have stuffed in your heart.
And all that stuff is keeping you from loving God the way He
wants us to and loving you the way He requires.

Refusing to love yourself is not an option. Loving yourself is a
command. Jesus said there is no greater commandment than
these: to love God with everything we have, love ourselves, and
love others. So, what happens when I don't love myself? I can't
love others. And it all starts with loving God. If I don't love God,
then there's already a breach in this because I'm limited on the
love I can extend.

There is a daughter or son right now who needs love, but their
mother or father or caregiver can't give it because they're limited
on the love they can extend. Why? Because they are bankrupt of
that love within themselves.

There is a husband right now who needs love from his wife,
but she can't give it because she doesn't love herself, nor does she

love God the way He requires us to. The love she can extend is limited since she is bankrupt of that love within.

There's a church member right now who needs love and guidance from a spiritual leader or pastor. Yet they're not getting it because of that pastor's or leader's hurt.

I'm limited on the love I can extend when my heart is bankrupt of that love.

There is a woman right now who needs love from her husband. But he can't love her the way God created him to because he lacks love for God and for himself.

The Bible backs this up. Ephesians 5:28 states, "In this same way, husbands ought to love their wives as their own bodies. He who loves his wife loves himself."

Say that backward: "He who loves himself loves his wife."

Is this hitting you hard? It sure did for me. This truth carries weight. Here's why:

I've been in church my whole life, but after thirty years, I had never heard a sermon on the idea of loving me, nor had someone ever sat me down and taught me this message from Scripture. I've never been discipled or given a biblical exegesis from this text on how to love me the way God tells me to. Don't get me wrong: It's easy to fall into the trap of loving ourselves in an arrogant, prideful way. However, I'm not talking about that kind of self-love. In fact, I think fear of arrogant self-love has kept us from talking about healthy self-love to the harm of many Christ followers. That said, I am here to tell you that God wants you to learn to love yourself more like He loves you.

I'm talking about the God-ordained love He desires for us to share with one another so that we can be lights in the world. I never saw teaching from the Scriptures on valuing myself or on the necessity of loving myself. I never even saw steps on *how* to love myself.

How many sermons have you heard on this? Has somebody ever sat down and talked to you about loving the process of who you are becoming versus shaming yourself for who you have been?

We need to learn to love the process, to love the wilderness. You must learn to love being chiseled and love when things in your life are falling off. All of this will make you the version of you that God wants you to be—the best version.

An example of this was when my wife was expecting our first child. Suddenly, things in her life began to shift. Her appetite changed. The activities she could or couldn't do changed. All of this was transforming her into a mom. She was carrying a gift and a blessing, yet it was making her nauseous. This was the process of becoming a new version of herself. It was uncomfortable for her to navigate, but it was part of her process. And because she was able to lean into and learn from this season, it was ultimately a blessing and led to her flourishing.

How might you lean into the season God currently has you in? When we trust that God is always at work to grow our faith, we can lean into the seasons He brings to learn from them and grow in His grace.

So many times, we mislabel pain and love. God is chiseling you so you can love like He loves, but many of us call that rebuke. I'm not trying to minimize church hurt, but so often, the source of that hurt wasn't truly a church—just because it said "Jesus Christ" on the doorpost or had "Christ" in its name doesn't mean Jesus was there. Most of us have never been taught from Scripture how to love ourselves while we're in the process of becoming instead of shaming ourselves for our pasts. The shame you are carrying will not lead to your healing or growth. God needs to cut that away.

Now that I understand more of this, I've learned that I love me better with standards, boundaries, and discipline. I love me better with obedience. I love this version of me better when I keep my word to myself. And I do that because I've learned to keep my word to God.

There's a fulfillment that comes when you tell yourself you're going to run or work out that day and then you do it. Follow-through leads to fulfillment. That is a better version of yourself.

I love the version of me that cherishes God's Word, because there was a time when I didn't care about the gospel. Now I cherish the gospel because I understand it is the original plan God had for my life. His desire was for me to be close to Him, to dwell with Him. We lost that in the Garden of Eden, yet now through the gift of salvation, I can reclaim this by being redeemed by my Redeemer.

All this doesn't make me think more highly of myself than I ought. I am simply choosing to believe the same things about myself that God does. The self-love that culture teaches is all about you. But loving yourself so you can love your neighbors is loving what God loves. It is self-love with a purpose. Loving ourselves like God loves us empowers us to love our neighbors more and trains us to treat them with respect. When you learn to love and respect yourself like God does, you will find yourself growing more generous toward the people around you. Furthermore, when you truly respect yourself, you'll be better positioned to represent the kingdom of light in the midst of a world that promotes darkness.

"Do not think of yourself more highly than you ought" (Romans 12:3). You need to choose—and *choose* is the key word—to think the same thoughts about yourself that the Most High does.

Consider what 1 Peter 2:9 says about you:

> You are a chosen people, a royal priesthood, a holy nation, God's special possession, that you may declare the praises of him who called you out of darkness into his wonderful light.

God tells us to remember that we are chosen by Him, that we are royalty. Thinking these things is not arrogant; it's so that we may praise the One who brought us out of darkness and into His wonderful light.

"Once you were not a people, but now you are the people of God; once you had not received mercy, but now you have received mercy" (verse 10). I choose to believe this about myself. God chose me. God gave me mercy. God loves me.

And what better verse than this one shows how much He loves me? "God so loved the world, that he gave his only begotten Son, that whosoever believeth in him should not perish, but have everlasting life" (John 3:16, kjv).

GOD SAVES YOU FROM THINGS BECAUSE HE'S SAVING YOU FOR THINGS

As someone who used to verbally abuse myself, I have learned the power of rephrasing my self-talk. Think of it this way: The Bible has much to say on how we talk about other people—we must not lie to them (Colossians 3:9) or slander them (1 Peter 2:1)—so don't talk about yourself that way either. So many of us are stuck in spirals of tearing ourselves down that we've never stopped to think that we fit into the category of people God calls us to honor and bless with our words. Doing this has reshaped and reframed my perspective, which affects the way I am. Let's see how this works.

I CAN'T	I NEED MORE KNOWLEDGE AND PRACTICE
I'M NOT GOOD ENOUGH	JESUS IS THE GOOD, AND MY LIFE IS HID IN HIM
I'VE MADE SO MANY MISTAKES	MY PAST DOESN'T DETERMINE MY FUTURE
DID THEY LIKE THIS?	I'M RESPONSIBLE FOR MY OBEDIENCE, NOT THEIR HAPPINESS

Anytime I found myself saying, "I can't," as in I didn't have the skill to do something, I rephrased it to "What I need is more knowledge and practice." Reframing this affected the way I am.

Here's another example. Instead of "I'm not good enough," I rephrase it and say, "Jesus is the good, and my life is hidden in Him." Rephrased and reframed, it affects the way I am.

This is so important. I used to think that I didn't get some things because I wasn't good enough. But now I view this in a different way. When I don't get things in my life, I tell myself I won't compromise. *I would have to compromise to get that, and I'm not going to do that.* God has a way of saving you *from* things because He's saving you *for* things. Don't believe the lie that says you're not good enough, because Jesus is the good and your life is hidden in Him.

Do you catch yourself saying, "I've made so many mistakes"? Reframe that to "My past doesn't determine my future."

In fact, if you were to erase all your mistakes, you would also erase all the wisdom you've gained from them. So, take the wisdom. Eulogize the disappointment. Reframing and rephrasing affect who you are.

One last one: "Did they like this?" This is what a lot of pastors, leaders, and podcasters ask themselves. If your mind is orbiting around this question all day, you can become a slave to your applause. So, I rephrase it:

"I'm responsible for my obedience, not their happiness."

Your happiness is not my responsibility. Your joy can be found in God; it is not my responsibility. So, when I preach, serve, help others know more about Christ, walk with someone who has lost a loved one, or visit the sick, I do all these things out of obedience because this is what God called me and commissioned me to do. Do you see how freeing it is to know this calling and to demonstrate God's love for others by what I do?

We must obey and believe what God has said about us—not just for ourselves but also for our spouses and children. You can't tell your wife how proud you are of her when you don't even know how to say, "I'm proud of me." Remember what Ephesians 5:28 says: "Husbands ought to love their wives as their own bodies. He who loves his wife loves himself."

This was a game changer for me. It made me realize a startling truth:

If I don't believe I'm the head of the home and if I don't obey and believe what God said about me, my whole bloodline will feel that.

If you don't believe what God says about you, your spouse and children will feel it. Your friends and coworkers will feel it. Everybody you share your gift with will feel it when they get close to you.

This is something that helped me. I knew I had to get to a place where I viewed myself the same way God views me.

Nothing about me is self-made.

Everything about me is God-made.

This is why rejection hits some of us so hard. You rejected yourself long before they ever did, so their rejection is confirmation of your self-hatred! It's why many of us can tolerate toxicity. You curse yourself out!

Instead of doing that, pray the following prayer: "God, please purge me of not loving myself the way You love me. Teach me to love what You love. And You love me!"

GIVE YOURSELF GRACE SPACE TO FALL IN LOVE WITH BECOMING

As we close out this journey of looking to God to rehabilitate our hearts, I want to stress that it is a journey, a process. Your heart certainly won't heal overnight, nor will you automatically and instantaneously become the person God made you to be. While this might feel discouraging, here is the good news: You can start taking legitimate strides toward healing now, and it begins with falling in love with the process of becoming. So, how do you get to a place where you see yourself the way God sees you? I will give you ten ways.

1. Discover what God says about you

Here's an easy homework assignment: I want you to open your Bible and then make a list of eight passages where God says something about you. Eight is a great number, because it is the number for new beginnings. Find eight Bible verses where God is expressing some truth about you, and write them down. When negative thoughts come, resist them with the words you wrote down. Arm yourself with multiple scriptures so that when you or somebody else says something to tear you down, you can combat those words with the Word of God.

When Jesus was tempted by Satan, how did He fight back? He kept saying, "It is written." Jesus was revealing to us how to engage in spiritual warfare and how to cast out damaging thoughts.

2. Rehearse God's thoughts toward you instead of your own

Meditate on God's thoughts about you. Look at what God says about David.

I've noticed that when the Lord referenced David in 1 Kings, He called him "righteous and upright in heart" (3:6) and said he walked before Him "faithfully with integrity of heart and uprightness" (9:4). Did He constantly mention Bathsheba? No. God called David his righteous, upright, faithful servant without adding anything about David's past sins.

Why didn't God mention Bathsheba? It's because He forgave David! So, if God forgave David and He's forgiven you of your sins, why are you still punishing yourself?

3. Stop the verbal abuse

It's time to end the verbal abuse of yourself. What happens when you keep speaking that language of abuse? It's almost like you're writing on a mirror. Every single time you look in the mirror, you see those words you called yourself:

> *Mean.*
> *Prideful.*
> *Liar.*
> *Sorry.*
> *Not enough.*

When you view yourself this way, you can't see how God sees you, because you see yourself through the lens and the reflection of your own thoughts and words.

4. Speak life

What do your words reveal about your heart? And who hears those words when you say them?

Psalm 103:20–21 says, "Bless the LORD, you His angels, who excel in strength, who do His word, heeding the voice of His word. Bless the LORD, all you His hosts, you ministers of His, who do His pleasure" (NKJV). David is pointing out that angels can hear God's word.

Now let's look at an example of this in Daniel 10:12, where an angel said, "Do not be afraid, Daniel. Since the first day that you set your mind to gain understanding and to humble yourself before your God, your words were heard, and I have come in response to them." The angel had heard the words Daniel prayed and had come to him in response.

So, if angels can hear your words, so can demons, who are fallen angels. I wonder if this is one of the multifaceted reasons why Proverbs 18:21 says, "Death and life are in the power of the tongue, and those who love it will eat its fruit" (NKJV).

What words are you speaking that can be heard in the spirit realm? And if they came back to you, would it be from the heavenly host or from a demonic spirit? Speak life:

I'm the head, not the tail.
I'm forgiven; Grace dismissed my case.
There's no condemnation for those who are in Jesus.
My best days are ahead of me; the only things people can take from me now are notes.

Speak life.

5. Give space for grace

You had years of pumping yourself with toxicity. So, be patient with yourself as God is detoxing you. Give yourself grace so you can fall in love with becoming who God calls you to be, instead of shaming yourself for who you have been. Consider how much you've grown. What if this hurtful thing had happened two years ago? How would you have felt and reacted? Now you know that God has something better for your life. What if you had received this bad report in the past? You would have lost your peace, but now you're praying over it. Do you see the growth?

6. Know the power of no

You're going to say no a whole lot more when you know your assignment. When you don't know your assignment, distractions look like opportunities. It's the power of no.

Here's a practical example. A friend recently came into town and asked if we could have lunch. The only time he could do it was when I was recording my Therapy Thursday, so I had to tell my friend no. When you know your assignment, you can identify distractions and know what you must do. It's when we're unclear of our assignment or task that we begin to say yes to the things we should say no to.

7. Reward the becoming

I've talked a lot in this book about how there is a version of you that God desires and designed you to be. Growth is the process of becoming that person. So, when I see that happening in my own life, here's something I've been doing: reward the becoming.

Say I read my Bible twenty days straight—I'm celebrating that!

Yes, I'm serving my church well and am faithful with God's Word.

There's a hatred of sin brewing up in me.

God, thank You for changing me!

Reward the person God is molding you to be versus continuously spotlighting the person you used to be.

8. Recognize what isn't your business

They don't like my calling? That's not my business.

What they think of me? That's not my business either.

Their response to me? That's none of my business.

What I'm doing is out of obedience to God. What they're doing or thinking is none of my business.

9. Rest

Some of you don't like yourselves because you're mentally exhausted. You can't see all the work God is doing in you because you're looking only through the lens of "I'm tired."

Maybe you don't need to quit—you just need a nap!

What are *naps*? They are *necessary adult peace sessions*.

So, take a nap and get some rest!

10. Engage in godly recreation

The last point is that you must have recreation. Life was not meant to be tormenting. Yes, there are evil practices in this world that grieve me, but I must be able to bond and have community.

We need to have godly recreation. When you set out to have fun, consider how you might do so in a way that honors God and leads to your good and the good of your neighbor. You don't have to get high or drunk to have a good time. You also don't have to win every card game or every pickup basketball game—if the way you play games is causing people to not want to play with you, it might be time to consider whether your approach to recreation is godly. Godly recreation means bearing the fruit of the Spirit (Galatians 5:22–23) in the way you play, compete, and relax.

Some of us don't know how to have kingdom recreation! We need to enjoy a kingdom community where we can lock arms with our brothers and sisters and enjoy the life and beauty God has given us.

Remember, God calls you to love Him, to love yourself, and to love others. The only version of you that can carry out God's command is the loving-me version.

CONCLUSION

We've come a long way together. From examining the problematic patterns that keep us stuck to learning how to quiet our crowded minds. From battling worst-case scenarios to surrendering our desires for control. From recognizing spiritual warfare to healing after painful breakups. All of these chapters have been pointing to one central truth:

God wants to rehabilitate your heart so you can become who He created you to be.

When I started Therapy Thursday, I had no idea how many people were walking around with shattered hearts, trying their best to hide the brokenness inside. I've seen firsthand how untreated trauma can shape our perspectives, cloud our decisions, and steal our joy. But I've also witnessed the transformational power of allowing God to be the Great Physician of our hearts.

Looking back at our journey through this book, I want to remind you of some truths we've uncovered:

You are God-made, not self-made. Everything about you was crafted by the Creator of the universe. He doesn't make mistakes, and He didn't make one with you.

The problem is often the pattern, not the person. Many of us try to change locations when we should be changing behaviors. We try to treat symptoms without addressing the root causes.

Your mind is a battlefield, and what you feed it matters. The voices you listen to will move you either toward God's purpose or away from it.

Red flags are warnings, not invitations. God loves you too much to let you wander into harm without warning signs.

It's not personal; it's spiritual. So much of what we experience is part of a larger battle that we can't see with our natural eyes.

You can't love others as yourself if you don't first love yourself as God loves you. This isn't prideful; it's acknowledging the value God places on you.

I know that change doesn't happen overnight. Heart rehabilitation is a process. There will be days when you fall back into old patterns, when those crowded thoughts return, and when worst-case scenarios seem more real than God's promises. That's okay. Give yourself grace space.

Remember what I said: God is not cutting you to hurt you; He's cutting you to keep you. He's not putting you through pain to punish you. He's allowing discomfort to develop you.

Now it's time for you to step out—to take what you've learned and begin applying it to your life. Start small. Pick one area we've discussed that resonated most deeply with you, and focus there. Maybe it's examining the patterns that keep showing up in your life. Maybe it's quieting your mind so you can hear God's voice more clearly. Maybe it's learning to love yourself the way God loves you.

Whatever you choose, know this: You don't have to do it alone. The same Holy Spirit who guided me to write these words will guide you as you read them. He'll show you what areas need attention, what wounds need healing, and what truths need reinforcing.

There's a version of you that God has destined you to become. A version that's free from the chains of past trauma. That doesn't overthink or catastrophize. That trusts God's plan and surrenders control. That discerns spiritual realities and handles relationships with wisdom. It's a version of you that loves God, loves yourself, and loves others from a place of wholeness.

That version of you is waiting on the other side of your heart rehabilitation.

So, let me ask you one more time:

Do you still want to say, "I don't want to be like this"?

Or are you ready to say, "God, make me like *You*"?

The choice is yours. The journey is yours. And your heavenly Father is waiting with open arms to walk with you every step of the way.

Your heart rehab starts now.

QUESTIONS

1. How would you complete this sentence: "I don't want to be _____ anymore"? What version of you is God calling you to become instead?

2. Which of the ten ways to see yourself as God sees you resonates most with you? How can you begin implementing a greater awareness of this in your daily life?

3. What verbal abuse have you been directing at yourself? What God-given truths can you speak over yourself instead?

4. How can you begin giving yourself "grace space" to fall in love with the process of becoming who God created you to be?

PRAYER

God, thank You for loving me. Please help me stop listening to the lies of the enemy. Help me release whoever the offender was. The forgiveness I give them is not about their innocence but about Your forgiveness. Help me also understand that forgiveness does not always mean reentry. The wisdom that I gain, I need. So, Lord, give me the wisdom. I know it's not Your will for me to go through pain from ignorance in order to get wisdom. If I go through pain, let it be purposeful suffering that can bring me closer to You versus my ignorance and my disobedience.

Oh, God, for that brother or sister who has tears in their eyes and who is battling suicidal or defeated thoughts, I pray peace will start to invade their heart. I pray that they begin to see themselves maybe for the first time through Your lens and not the lens of their failures, mistakes, and shortcomings. Let them know that the cross and Your blood is enough. In Jesus's name we pray, amen.

BONUS CONTENT

To continue rehabbing your heart, use your smartphone to scan the code for a bonus video diving deeper into the content of this chapter.

URL: waterbrookmultnomah.com/HRChapterTen

ABOUT THE AUTHOR

JERRY FLOWERS JR. and his wife, Tanisha Flowers, are the founders of Redefined TV and are passionate about redefining relationships righteously. With numerous videos that have gone viral on YouTube, Instagram, TikTok, and Facebook, along with four cross-country tours, these generational pacesetters are dedicated to allowing their marriage and ministry to be a stage from which people can see Jesus and a healthy model of kingdom ministry. The Flowers are based in Houston, Texas, and are lead pastors at Time of Celebration Ministries Church. They are the proud parents of three beautiful children, Melody, Jerry III, and Josiah.

ABOUT THE TYPE

This book was set in Dante, a typeface designed by Giovanni Mardersteig (1892–1977). Conceived as a private type for the Officina Bodoni in Verona, Italy, Dante was originally cut only for hand composition by Charles Malin, the famous Parisian punch cutter, between 1946 and 1952. Its first use was in an edition of Boccaccio's *Trattatello in laude di Dante* that appeared in 1954. The Monotype Corporation's version of Dante followed in 1957. Though modeled on the Aldine type used for Pietro Cardinal Bembo's treatise *De Aetna* in 1495, Dante is a thoroughly modern interpretation of that venerable face.